I have a story for you ...

Volume Two

by:

Carole Bertuzzi Luciani

ISBN: 978-0-9919100-0-7

Cataloguing data available from Library and Archives Canada.

For information: www.moodivatior.ca or
www.carolebertuzziluciani.com

First edition
Published and printed in Canada

People, places or incidents mentioned and/or information provided
herein reflect solely the author's viewpoint. Any resemblance to actual
persons, living or dead, business establishments, events, or locales is
entirely coincidental or based solely on the author's perspective.

Library and Archives Canada registration admin
and production management through the
TRI Publishing™ program
TRIMATRIX Management Consulting Inc.
www.trimatrixmanagement.com

Setting the Tone

Life is about the stories we tell; our favourite times with family and friends happen when we sit around the table swapping stories. Sometimes the details are faded, the memory a bit off or a new version might emerge but that's what brings us together, entertains us, touches us and somehow gently massages our heart.

Since the publishing of *I have a story for you* ... Volume One, I have learned a lot. We all have stories we've heard, ones we've lived and ones we want to share. I've learned that once you break the seal to your own writing a plethora of memories and magic is revealed; and I learned that no goal is insurmountable.

When I witnessed the delivery of three giant vacuum-sealed pallets containing my first book being dropped at the end of my driveway, a wave of dread engulfed me. It could have been that the driver was reluctant to transport them into my house even though it was raining. And it didn't help that at one point he stopped, sighed heavily and proclaimed, "I need to stop and take my blood pressure pill. Impatiently, I muttered, "Can I have one of those?"

Suddenly I realized the magnitude of my goal to sell 5000. Being self-published, I knew there would be no press machine behind me and I had no world-wide notoriety. Lacking any previous literary experience, I quickly recognized that it would be me selling them one book at a time. The reality of it all poked me right in the gut. What was I thinking?

Thanks to my inherent stubbornness and tenacity I set out to meet that goal. Book signing events were plenty and proved to be one of the most humbling experiences. Typical attempts at connecting with a potential buyer included such chit-chat as:

"Can I interest you in a good book?"

"NO."

In my mind ... "Okay. Then go help yourself to a bad one."

"Hi, can I tell you about my book?"

"I don't read."

In my mind ... "Hmm, but you're in Chapters. Perhaps you've landed in the wrong store."

After numerous futile attempts I discovered my best opening line was "Can I interest you in a mediocre book?" Somehow I got their attention with that one.

I accepted speaking opportunities with hopes of selling copies of my book afterwards. At one such engagement, after I announced that I would love to sell them each a copy, an older woman stood up from the crowd of 25 and announced, "I'll be buying a book on behalf of all of us for the library. My treat."

But I never lost hope because after all, I knew early on it would be a best-seller. Here's why ...

Shortly after the book debuted I visited my mom to present her with her copy. Without looking at it she placed it on the dining room table and returned with a sales receipt, which she promptly dropped in my hand. "Go to Zellers for me. They overcharged me for the paper towels."

When I returned home Joe asked me what she thought of the book. I told him what happened and he was both annoyed and disappointed with her response.

A few days later he called her and asked, "Mom, how do you like Carole's book?"

She was quick to respond, "Oh I thought I'd wait to read it when I had some time." Other than the daily crossword I'm not sure what else my mom, who was 89, had pencilled in her day timer.

However, a few days later there was a message on our machine, which was unusual for her. "Well I thought I'd read just one story but there's something about this book that draws you in. I'm on page 110."

I immediately scanned through the index to see what truths she had already uncovered. Phew, I'd made it through almost half of the book unscathed.

The next day she left another message. "Well I finished the book. I have to tell you I'm really surprised. I really enjoyed it."

Upon hearing her testimony I threw my hands up in the air and announced, "Joe, it's gonna be a best seller. She read it. She liked it. She wants copies for her friends. Cool the champagne, baby!"

Eventually Volume One did earn Canadian Best- Seller status with 5000 + copies sold. No, I have not received a congratulatory message from the Queen, an invitation to be a part of Oprah's Book Club or even a call from Heather of Chapters fame. The truth is that other than my valued family and friends not many even know about it, but that's okay.

For this book, I chose to print a limited number of copies. I will be embarking on a different journey this time. One that will certainly take up less of my time and energy and demand less from my creative marketing mind. That means my intention is to put it in the hands of those who know me ... no more book signings, no more random mailings in hopes of it being reviewed and definitely no feeling the pressure to get it out there.

Volume Two is like what my Nona called her special recipes, all prepared with love and the perfect blend ingredients of "a little bit o' this, a little bit o' that."

Some stories have been collecting cyberspace dust in my old computer files, some have been taken directly from my blogs over the past few years and others have been freshly written and never before shared.

My intent with each is that you will react with pleasure ... a gentle grin, a slight grimace, hearty smile or even a wholesome belly laugh.

I hope you will appreciate the writing in the spirit intended ... to touch your heart, to make you think and to ultimately tickle your funny bone.

Enjoy~!!~

Your Reading List

Dedicated ... with Gratitude

In Volume One, my tribute was to the three most prominent individuals in my life. They know who they are.

For this book I choose to dedicate it to my family and friends, many of whom are characters in my stories.

You are the ones I happily share my life adventures with ... the laughs, the love and all the lessons along the way. May it continue to be a pleasure for all of us.

A Treasured Book Review

$\mathcal{W}$riting a book is the easy part of being an author ... the real challenge is selling it. This is a chronic and sometimes painful part of the process which can easily plant debilitating thoughts of doubt in your mind: "Did I do the right thing? Is it good enough? Will I ever sell them all?"

But today I received something in the mail that erased all doubt. It arrived in a small white, handwritten, scotch-taped envelope with these thoughtful words that made my day ...

Thank you.

May 23 2011

Hi Carole,

I feel like I have known you all my life I just start reading your book which by the way I found in the library at work as you can see my spelling is not as good either
Where I found your book I work at ST Michael hospital I just red read the first chapter about your Nona and my co worker thinks I; m; out of my mind I was laughing out so loud
Tears running down my face I know I will enjoy the rest of the book and I will past it on to my next laughter/reader

Thank you

God bless you
Thank you for my therapy

The Kitchen Table

*L*ike most families in the 1950's we owned one table that serviced most of our needs. It had an arborite top with a pearly gray and white swirled design and was framed in chrome. Some wealthier families enjoyed that same style only upgraded in more colourful hues.

Unlike today's home decor, with only having only one table, made it the focal point. It was *home base*, where all colouring, homework and reading the paper occurred; where my mom's sewing evolved as well as my dad's house drawings; where airplane models were assembled, cards were dealt and Monopoly was played; where discipline took place, secrets shared, announcements made and when Nona visited, homemade pasta was rolled. But regardless which activity was going on, it all got cleared away when it was time to eat.

Our kitchen table was small, and barely fit the five of us but we still ate every family meal there together whether in harmony or not. I can't tell you how many glasses of milk were spilled on it resulting in some form of punishment, verbal or otherwise. As well it was the home base for our consumption of way too many calories from food we'd never consider eating today. And depending on where you sat, some of that food landed in the small drawer of the table for future retrieval.

When company came over we easily made room around it for any extra bodies. And if no more chairs would fit, the kids would stand behind leaning on the shoulders of their parents. Sure, it had an extension but when pulled out, the ends sat half an inch below the rest of the tabletop. This defect was solved by laying the tablecloth to both cover it up and if needed, dress it up ... we just had to remember where the disjointed seam was so the platters didn't tip. But it really never seemed to matter because the more people crammed around the table, the more fun the meals were.

When we moved to another home, unfortunately that table remained in place as part of the buying price. We had to adjust to a more upgraded version of it for our new home. As well, we had to invest in a dining room table, mainly because we acquired a dining room in the process. Interestingly, that table was reserved for special occasions only.

Years later I was comforted when I met Joe's parents and saw they owned that *same* table nicely settled in their kitchen. Fully grown by then, my legs no longer fit beneath it but it still felt just right ... the tilt of the extension, the small pull-out drawer and the chilled temperature of the chrome against my bare skin. As we sat around and shared table tales, I learned that fish had been shucked on it, money lost in poker games most Friday nights and it was where Joe's mom cut all of her patterns. And most intriguing, it was where Joe's tonsils were removed.

After the deaths of Joe's parents, I was pleased to inherit it for our own home.

Now when a visitor sees that table in our basement it immediately tweaks nostalgic reminders of their past and a smile emerges ... "Oh, wow. *We* had that table ...."

Hmm, I wonder if years from now, my kids will be able to recall what our current table looks like. Somehow I doubt it.

P.S. To preserve the special memory, that wonderful table was photographed for the background of both of my book covers.

Gramma in the Slamma

We grew accustomed to hearing stories about our grandmother, Nona. She arrived in Canada from Italy when she was seven, went to Grade One but after just a few months was sent to work in the cotton mill in Hamilton. She was the second youngest of eight.

By fourteen she was pursued by a family friend twelve years older. Though reluctant to commit, she married him. At one time she revealed that she felt she had to, because he had bought her a pair of red shoes. She thought she owed him. Their life together was as volatile as it was eventful.

We relished hearing her tell tales. Family members continued to share them well after her death. Although some were told repeatedly there was one story that only surfaced on rare occasions. Perhaps it was because it was never validated by my own mother. And because of that there were numerous variations of the same event.

During the Great Depression in the late 1920's when most were unemployed, many received *relief* and all would do anything to make ends meet for their families. Nona too, did what she could to provide for her family. She was a bootlegger. She serviced her friends and apparently the local police as well.

It wasn't so much her newly acquired profession that proved to be problematic but what she did to defend it and herself.

One Saturday evening my grandparents did what they most enjoyed … entertaining *paesani* (friends) and *famiglia* (family) in *casa* (in their home). It was certain there would be delicious Italian cooking and although the prohibition was on, as a bootlegger Nona could also provide them with booze. Whether or not payment was made, (those facts are no longer available to me), the rest of the story is …

At some point in the night amidst the roaring voices of the crowd a cop entered their home in the north end of Hamilton. Normally *her friends in the force* were able to tip her off to any surprise visits, however on this particular night the message had not been received. Looking around it was obvious what was taking place among the party-goers as it was a common occurrence in those days. The guilty charge was automatic with the first sniff of alcohol.

But it wasn't being caught that pressed Nona's button and for certain gave her *agitto* (acid indigestion) and apparently she and the cop knew each other and the history they shared did not sit well with her. She really didn't like him. He was arrogant and a smart alec who took advantage of his position and bullied the likes of Nona and her north end community of immigrants.

In the process of dealing with the bootlegging issue he made a disparaging comment directly to and about my grandmother. Incited, she was not prepared to take *that* from anyone regardless of badge or brawn. She reached for her purse and took a swing at the man in uniform, hitting him across the head and knocking his esteemed hat to the ground.

Although some details of what followed had faded, the truth recently emerged. Just this past Christmas my mother finally confirmed that the story was factual. Nona was handcuffed and transported to a cell, on an upper floor of Hamilton's Barton Street Jail.

My mother then recalled how her father walked all of the children down the street from their home, stood at the corner of Barton and Ferguson Avenue, and said: "Look up there. Wave to your mother. She's on the third floor."

She was to stay in jail for two weeks but when her case was presented before the judge she got out earlier than planned.

Apparently, he had been a customer.

That's our Nona … that's why we loved her.

Going a Few Rounds

I enjoy studying the differences between men and women … not just physically, but mostly about how we behave. Specifically, I am fascinated by how we communicate.

When Joe and I are together, perhaps at a mall, inevitably one of his 356,000 students from the past will come out of nowhere and excitedly blurt, "Hey Mr. Luciani, How are ya doing?"

Now, I know within 11 seconds if Joe has an iota of a clue of who the person is. Once I determine this, I will either excuse myself, interject to introduce myself or step away and eavesdrop on the conversation while people watching.

What I have discovered in doing the latter is that over the course of the next seven minutes of their engaged conversation, all that really is accomplished or learned is this: they will proceed to ask each other 'how they are' in a multitude of ways.

Typically, I will overhear chatter that includes:

"Hey, how ya' doin'?

"Good. Good. How you doin'?"

"Great. So how have you been?"

"Not bad. How's everything with you?'

"Oh, I can't complain. Life treating you well?"

"Heck yeah. Everything's good. So what's up?"

"Not much. Anything new with you?"

"Hey. It was great talking to you. So nice to catch up."

I think you get the gist.

But somehow as women we converse in a completely different pattern. We waste no time at all before get down and dirty gathering as much information as possible in record speed and time.

I call this classic scenario Going A Few Rounds:

Upon meeting up with a friend in a parking lot, the dialogue might go something like this (supported by an imaginary dinger bell) …

"Oh my goodness. Jane. It's you. How are you? (screeching the words into her right ear as I squeeze her tightly). Wow, we have to catch up. Between us there is just too much history …"

DING

"I just had a hysterectomy. I'm on a personal rejuvenation program … I've had my veins pulled, my eyes lasered. Only thing left is I have to do something about my teeth. I have this gap …"

DING

"I was at The Gap just the other day. I had to return a sweater I got from the kids for Christmas. While I was standing there, out of the corner of my eye I caught a glimpse of the display of jeans. It reminded me of the show I saw about the jeans that look good on everyone. I think they're called Long and Lean …"

DING

"Lean hamburger meat's on sale at Longos. I noticed it the other day when I went to the hairdressers …"

DING

"Oh I finally found the name of my old hairdresser. I'm so relieved. He's the only one who knows my hair. I can't believe he landed back in Oakville …"

DING

"We're looking at houses in Oakville, but the prices of real estate are sooo high ..."

DING

"My youngest came home high the other night and it was all I could do to hold myself from kicking him back out ..."

DING

"Oh, you know my cousin came out last summer eh? He's going to have an intimate wedding in our garden ..."

DING

"You don't know the name of a good gardener, do you? I've got this one little spot ..."

DING

"My gosh. Did Ted find your g-spot? My husband needs directions ..."

DING

"Aren't those GPS's annoying ... recalculating, this route will now take an extra five minutes ..."

DING

"Yikes. Look at the time ... gotta go for a pap smear."

And as I turn to leave the embrace, we can be heard yelling,

"Hey and let me know how your mammogram goes."

We leave feeling completely rejuvenated but with our heads spinning. Upon returning home I might say, "Joe I ran into Jane today."

"Oh yeah. What's new with her?"

"Nothing."

Humbled Once Again

As a staff member at Camp Tawingo in Huntsville I learned that working could be fun and in such an accepting environment the wackier you were, the better. During my stints of employment there I had the chance to do a variety of jobs with numerous opportunities to be a part of the daily zany antics. Even in my adult years, I continued to spend a few weeks there each summer to get my camp fix.

One year I especially enjoyed my position as librarian, creating an inviting space for campers and staff to drop by, snag a book or a board game and hang out. As part of the role, I was responsible for running all of the tournaments from Checkers to Risk, with some competitions attracting hundreds of entrants. It all culminated before the final banquet, when the winners were announced, invited to the stage and handed their homemade awards.

I hadn't been on stage yet that summer and typically it was an nerve wracking experience. Even though I was used to speaking in front of large audiences, for some reason taking the stage at camp to face 500 youthful faces belonging to both campers and staff, was unnerving. It didn't help that everyone who ever stepped up on that stage was extremely polished as they displayed their skills in drama, music and humour.

The banquet day agenda of events was long and I was slated to acknowledge my winners immediately following lunch. I knew I'd have to be quick and to the point. Feeling a bit anxious, I headed off to the washroom before the announcements began.

I returned to my spot at the back of the room, where I frequently sat with my friend Jane, just before the intros started. We chose that table because of its distance from the *area of influence* at the front, where most of the other staff sat and because it was a closer trip to the kitchen for the food.

I anxiously waited to be introduced. When I finally heard my name, I quickly weaved my way to the front between a number of tables. I stepped up onto the stage and turned towards the mic to begin. But directly in front was my friend Jane kneeling on the floor below. I was puzzled … why was she there? Why had she trailed after me on her knees? And why was she staring up at me with the look of a hungry dog? Although baffled I couldn't pause to think about it because I had to start speaking. And as I did, she uttered a few "pssts" and flashed me a nervous smile that indicated she really had something important to tell me.

Not quite getting it, but determined to get the job done, I looked at her, smiled and continued my announcement. Jane remained crouched in front of me as she gestured intermittently. Because I didn't know what else to do, I continued talking, straining my voice to be heard over the howls of laughter from the audience. This, too, unnerved me because I knew I had not yet been funny.

From the front table, one of the senior staff finally signalled something to me. Still talking and doing my best to remain engaged with the audience I squinted to grasp what he was trying to tell me (somehow that helps with my hearing).

Uh oh. In a split second I got it. During my trip to the washroom a strip of used toilet paper had somehow missed the toilet and caught onto the back of my underwear, then over the waistband of my shorts thus creating a white (slightly soiled) tail behind me. Only as I reached back, did I feel the accessory loosely affixed to my belt loop.

To save myself (and my dignity), I quickly snatched it. And without missing a word from my announcement, I muttered, "Oh good, I was looking for that" as I nonchalantly crumpled it and jammed it into my pocket.

Jane remained in her crouched position on the floor, holding her sides to prevent them from erupting. Although the rest of the senior staff seated nearby looked sympathetic, they too seemed to be struggling to contain their composure.

I smoothly managed to redirect everyone's attention as the winners were awarded to a great round of applause. Confidently (never let them see you sweat) I returned to my seat as Jane crawled dignifiedly behind. It wasn't until I reached the bosom of my friends at the back of the room that we lowered our heads and laughed into our hands until the tears came.

I can only hope the younger audience had assumed it was all just part of the stage act.

The Gold Brick

I love having a nugget to gnaw on ... perhaps gleaned from a story I read, something shared in conversation, or even words woven into a sermon at church. It doesn't have to be much, anything to make me stop and think.

It happened one day at Mass. I don't remember the readings but for the first time in years the priest actually got my attention with his comments. He introduced his sermon with a story he called *The Gold Brick*. Although his version was brief I will elaborate for you. It went something like this:

A middle aged man had passed away and found himself at the pearly gates. He was met by St. Peter, the welcoming one who served as both greeter and majordomo of Heaven. He introduced himself as John Smith, was verified on the list and invited through.

As St. Peter eyed him closely, he asked John to wait until St. Julian, the patron saint of hospitality showed up. As John waited he looked around at all the beauty and splendor and was impressed that he actually had made it there, the coveted destination of his faith.

St. Julian arrived and announced that he would take John on a quick tour eventually ending up at his final home. As they walked, John loved what he saw. He was so excited he couldn't wait to see where his resting place would be. As they approached a hill John's eye went to the peak where he saw the most magnificent gold brick palace he had ever seen. Having worked in land development and real estate on earth, John knew architecture and he knew opulence. That gold brick structure was spectacular. St. Thomas, patron saint of builders had achieved award-winning status with that one.

They continued walking and St. Julian announced it would just be a few more minutes until they got to John's spot. They reached the top of the hill and seeing the awesome building up close, John couldn't stop ogling. He was impressed. But they kept walking and headed down the other side of the hill and around the bend.

Suddenly they stopped and St. Julian extended his arm as he announced, "John this is where you will remain. You have wonderful neighbours and are invited to enjoy all of the amenities. I certainly hope you will be happy here."

John was stunned at what he saw. His mouth dropped as he gawked at his new home, a structure so modest in appearance that it was little more than some flimsy plywood draped with heavy canvas and it leaned slightly to the right. To John it was really no more than a shoddy lean-to. He was so disappointed he was compelled to comment. "Excuse me St. Julian. I don't mean to be disrespectful but there must be some mistake here. You must not know who I am or the status I enjoyed while on earth."

"Indeed I do know all about you. It says right here you were a very successful businessman, made numerous investments, earned a lot of money and were held in high esteem for your wealth."

"That's all correct. So why is it that I will be stuck living in a rundown mess like this? Why can't I live up in that beautiful palace which is much more fitting for me?"

St. Julian shook his head in disagreement. "I'm sorry but that place is occupied."

"Well who can possibly be more deserving of that structure than me?"

"A gentleman named Mike Goodheart lives there."

"Whoa! Mike Goodheart my property manager? The guy who took care of my place, my cars and all of my needs before he passed away?"

"Yes, that's correct. That's him."

"I don't get it."

St. Julian was quick to explain. "John we have our own investment system on earth. For every good deed, act of goodwill, volunteer effort or community service extended, you earn a gold brick for your ultimate home in Heaven. Mike spent most of his free time giving of himself to others and his community, continually working to better the lives of those around him thus earning him enough gold bricks to erect his palace. Truthfully my friend, although you were a solid, reputable person, you were so concerned with making money and spending it that you amassed next to no resources for your ultimate home."

At that point in the sermon, Alena, who was nine at the time, leaned over and whispered, "Mommy, that means Noni (my father) is going to be living in a mansion when he dies."

That resonated in me for weeks. It nudged me to get more involved and give myself away more often ... like my father did most of his life. Although some of you may not believe in the concept of heaven or even saints, in your own way, you also frequently earn gold bricks. Some are small random acts, some are regular volunteer commitments and many are willing agreements to get involved in something other than your own life. Way to go. It's the giving of your time, energy, talents or even cash that makes our world better.

Critter with a Sweet Tooth

The panic call came in early and the only words I could make out from the meek and terrified voice of my mom on the other end were, "Carole, I have a mouse. How quickly can you get here to catch it?"

Surely she was kidding. It's not like I can call out to him, "Psst, over here" and he'll heed my command, come out of hiding, stroll up to me and present himself.

So of course with a quick assessment of the situation I deferred the task of Mouse Patrol to Joe. Dutifully he set off to appease my worried mom.

When he returned home he gave the report … apparently my mom figured that the mouse ate six packs of Mentos. I'm thinking, "My goodness that's one honkin' not-to-mention greedy mouse." But my mom swears it was true because there were exactly six packages the day before where only the wrappings remained.

Joe headed off to Canadian Tire, purchased the goods and returned to my mom's. With the traps set, the nerves were soothed and her mind put to rest that the unwelcome guest would be taken care of (but you know if there's one, there are always more … they're family oriented).

Next morning Joe was beckoned to check the progress, as she dare not peek, (it must be genetic). And to his surprise there lay snagged … the intruder. Joe reported that, although a toothache was the presumed cause of death, his breath remained sweet.

The Prairie Reception

For our post-university cross-Canada trip, my friend Nancy and I willingly agreed to drive our prof's car to BC, a gesture that benefitted all of us. He got his car delivered to his new home and we had free transportation for the first leg of our adventure.

It was a vintage VW Fastback, circa 1965 with lots of mileage and a gear stick not prepared for our rugged 'n rookie styled shifting. It made for an interesting ride. Our only major breakdown occurred as we entered Alberta. Recognizing something wasn't right that had little to do with our driving, we figured it would be best to pull off the Trans Canada in search of a repair shop. We were directed to a village called Youngstown, forty miles north and were told there was a small shop there that could handle a VW repair.

It was a good news/bad news scenario. We were assured they could easily correct the problem, however being close to shut down time for the staff of three, it would have to wait until morning. As we looked around the village, population 63, there was no evidence of a Motel 6, campground or a YWCA, all accommodations of choice. We asked where we might stay overnight.

"Ah, I reckon the best thing for you two young ladies to do is head over to the bar and meet some of the nice people of our area. I'm sure someone will put you up for the night."

Hmmm. Looking at each other with uncertainty, we winced, shrugged our shoulders and then reluctantly asked, "Which way?" With a quick jerk of his head we were out the door and onto the street looking for the meeting spot. We entered through the door with the sign *Visitors Welcome.*

Our entrance turned heads and solicited some smiles from the eclectic group occupying the bar stools. There were young guys wearing the grime of their day's work, older guys worn and rugged caressing their chilled beer, and women of all ages, just plain tough, studying us from head to toe. Clearly we were not from around there. If we were visiting the east coast our presence would have screamed, "We're from *away*."

It didn't take long for their small village curiosity to make friends with our eagerness to engage. After all, we were hoping to meet someone friendly and hospitable enough to offer their floor or couch to us for the night.

By the end of the evening, having consumed pitchers of cold draft and whatever the bar had to offer in food, all at no cost to us, we realized that we had not solved the problem of accommodation. Finally the young man from the gas station approached us and openly expressed it for us: "So where are you going to be staying tonight?"

What followed was open bidding as to who would be the lucky one to open their home to the two from the east. A quiet, soft spoken rancher named John interjected and explained he had plenty of room and he would be happy to provide an overnight place for us that included a ride back to retrieve our repaired vehicle.

As the night at the bar came to an end, Nancy and I found ourselves entering separate massive pick-ups driven by John and another rancher. At that point alcohol perhaps was a factor altering our better judgement. It seemed like forever that the half-ton truck sped along the dirt roads deeper into the prairies under the darkest of skies. I managed to maintain conversation with the stranger who would be our innkeeper but anxiously wondered and worried about the whereabouts of Nancy.

About an hour into the desolation of prairie ranch territory he pulled onto a long driveway. Although I was relieved to see his house I was even more elated to see Nancy and her driver pull in shortly after.

John showed us to our room and we said goodnight. Once we were safely behind the closed door we struggled to contain our nervous laughter: What the hell were we thinking leaving the bar with two strangers and then separating the way we did? We agreed it wasn't very smart and nothing was worth the worry we had just endured.

As we got ready for bed, we could hear the guys outside our room. By the sound of their voices it was obvious they had continued drinking. Nancy and I stared at each other with worried looks and immediately decided it might be best to go to bed … dressed.

Lying together in the same bed, we faced each other and whispered about how stupid we were, how the booze contributed to our misplaced trust and our bravery. And as we chatted to comfort each other, the noise outside our door increased. And the louder they got, the more aggressive they sounded. And the more aggressive they sounded the more scared we became. We immediately reached for our purses, wrapped them around our necks and positioned ourselves like spoons … if we were going down, we were going together.

We shared our concerns, our visions of the attacks, what they would do to us and how no one would know where we were. We were certain we'd never be found and would forever remain an unsolved murder mystery involving the two young girls from the east.

It took a few hours but as the noise settled we eventually fell asleep still clutching each other and only separated only by the bulk of our purses.

As the prairie sun filtered through the lace curtains, there was a gentle knock on the door. It was John: "Good morning girls. I hope we weren't too noisy for you last night and you slept well. I've made breakfast for you."

It suddenly dawned on us that we were not going to be today's news. In fact we had even slept. Surprisingly we had survived the night.

We called out to John that we'd be right there. And we were, because we were already dressed.

Entering the sun-filled farmhouse kitchen we saw that not only had he set the table, but had prepared a hearty breakfast of freshly hatched eggs and roasted chicken. His quiet, generous nature came to light. We learned about his family history, his ties to Youngstown and his passion for ranching. He toured us around his multi-acred property, prepared us to ride horses, taught us about badgers, told us about his closest neighbour five miles away and ultimately served as a true gentleman tour guide. As the morning wore on so did our guilt for convincing ourselves he was a dangerous criminal.

Fortunately the experience unfolded favourably for us. The car was repaired and we were released back in the direction of the Trans Canada Highway with a community send-off complete with hugs and best wishes.

Although elated with the hospitality extended to us by John and his friends we still had to question our own behaviour. What the hell had we been thinking and why were we so lucky to have come out unscathed?

P.S. I often think of that night and wonder how I would feel if my own daughter came home with a similar tale. YIKES!

Questionable Priorities or Not?

I was meeting with a group of women I didn't know very well to discuss an upcoming event we would all be involved in. Arriving late, a woman hurried in and before she could offer any pleasantries, she blurted out that their house had been broken into. Of course we were immediately concerned and whether we knew her or not, we wanted details.

She was quick to provide.

Yes, their beautiful home (in a pricey neighbourhood) had been burglarized and left in a state of disarray. Everything was upturned, china broken, jewelry stolen and it was obvious the intruders had thoroughly scoured through the contents of their home. Our reactions to her news were similar. We were both stunned and concerned.

But according to her that was not the worst of it.

Whoever broke in, not only stole some numerous valuables but also had found and taken her car keys.

A round of, "Oh-no's, OMG's" circulated as we fell back into our chairs, but there was more.

Not only had they stolen her treasured Mercedes but unfortunately she had been in a hurry that afternoon and had left her purse in the car.

At this we all gasped for air. We had heard stories like this but not happening to anyone we knew.

But she wasn't finished. According to her, although rightly upset by everything, she could handle all of that. But what followed was the breaking point of the story and clearly what was causing her the most distress.

She continued ...

"I have been floundering ever since my old hairdresser moved away a year and a half ago. I searched for him for months because he was the only one who really understood me and my hair. And finally the other day I found him. I was ecstatic. But his business card with all of his info was in my purse!!"

At this she broke down and cried.

My Memories of Thorold

*O*ur family lived in Thorold from 1952-1962. I believe I have not yet fully recovered from the move. Perhaps there is truth to the notion of packing valuable and intangible souvenirs when you leave a favourite place. The following is a sampling of the many great memories I treasure from that early part of my life ...

I loved the sights and sounds of the street from our home at 26 Whyte Avenue. The steady action of St. Charles School directly in front; the clanging of the flagpole with any trace of a wind; and the most magnificent playground a child could want in McMann Park ... all within my reach.

If we weren't playing allies on the boulevard, hide-'n-seek on the street or skipping on the driveway we were playing two ball against the wall at the back of the school. And when we tired of that we were resourceful to slip the same red, white

and blue ball into one leg of our Mom's nylon stockings. Who can forget the accompanying rhyme: *Hello, hello hello sir. Are you coming out sir ...?* We just had to remember to stay clear of the boys though as they whipped Indian Rubber balls against the wall retrieving them with their worn and flapping baseball gloves.

But the most fun was the park. It was there we extended our social circle beyond the kids on our block or in our class. It was the melting pot in our small town and it didn't matter where you lived or went to school. It was always *game on* and open to anyone willing to play.

The park had playground equipment we enjoyed with rigor, where mainstays, Eva and her sister would push us with great enthusiasm whether we wanted it or not. It was where I first learned that to teeter-totter properly required two people of equal weight. Sadly that rarely happened for me since I was considerably bigger than my friends. But, I finally learned that if I sat in front of the bar, all was well ... unless they of course jumped off as I was resting comfortably at the top. Ouch.

In the summer we had *playground* each morning where we met in circles and followed the lead of our friendly counsellors. And each afternoon we'd return to splash our time away in the wading pool and fight for control of the big drain in the deep end which I'm certain was no deeper than 18".

The highlight though, for us who lived within eyesight of the park was the annual parade of trailers that moved onto the grounds late each summer. That was when the carnival came to town and our freedom changed with its arrival. The rules were laid out by our parents, the warnings issued and promises made to obey. We were not to go there unaccompanied. They were the strangers we were to avoid.

However, it did not deter me when, at seven, I found thirty five cents and snuck over to the boats that flopped around a huge metal tub. Alone and eager to spend my stash I was so excited to enter the boats I didn't wait until they were completely stopped and ended up straddling one with a chubby leg in and another cold and wet. It was two nights later when my mom noticed the bruising that my adventure was exposed. Ouch again.

It was where I fell in love with baseball, watching endless games played by the boys. I would sit in the bleachers and stare at their uniforms, their spikes and oh how I loved the catcher's equipment. Secretly I knew I was good enough to join them, had they been agreeable to let girls play. After all, I had earned the tag Michelina Mantle on the pavement of Holy Rosary School. And it was there I was extended the invite to play Bird League with girls three years older.

Although our world seemed limitless we knew not to travel beyond the water tower on St. David's nor past Lock 7 at the canal where we only went when the ships sailed by, hoping the sailors would delight us with the tossing of their gob hats. Sullivan Park marked the other end where besides having the occasional Bird League game we definitely were there for fireworks. And beyond Collier Road, well that merely marked the beginning of the long (unaccompanied) bike ride along Beaver Dam Road to Decew Falls reserved for special outings only.

The truth is we basically travelled anywhere within those limits freely and without supervision. Our sole means of transportation was our CCM, most often purchased from Al's Cycle Shop where the scent of new bike and tire rubber filled the air. We'd decorate those bikes with streamers, mud flaps and assorted accessories that our meagre allowance would allow which usually meant baseball cards clothes pegged to our spokes. And regardless of how much pride we took in our bike we never thought to lock them or remove them from the front sidewalk at night.

My memories remain vivid of the various organized activities we enjoyed. There was the annual skating carnival when I was a Hawaiian dancer. But because there wasn't a hula skirt big enough to fit me … my mother had to make me one. We learned to swim at the *big pool* at McMillan Park with the dark blue walls which made it considerably more frightening than our little wading pool. And we bowled every Saturday

morning in a league which boasted my sister as its star, with a high score of 325. Heck I even took ballet from Miss Del Ben only to be made a tree for the recital while my sister Sharon and friend Teresa were the elegant flowers. The next year I took tap. And I can't forget the weekly Brownie meetings in the basement of the church next to the convent. I loved earning those badges.

It was at Holy Rosary where I had my first confession and after nervously lining up for my turn I forgot to use my inside voice resulting in a round of muffled laughter as I exited the curtained cubicle. First Communion followed and with a

bad case of the measles, a set of crooked teeth and a row of jagged bangs to match (I just couldn't sit still in the hairdresser's chair) I tried my best to be both solemn and joyful at the same time.

Our days in the classrooms of Holy Rosary revolved mostly around trying hard to obey the rules, stringently laid out by the nuns who taught us. It got to be too difficult a task for me as I was the one who solved the mystery of *Do nuns have hair?*

Sadly, I underestimated the length of my stride as well as the length of her veil. There, before our wondering eyes appeared the answer we had yearned for. A string of, "She's got hair. She's got hair. She's got hair." followed. Just one day later for the measly error in judgement of laughing into my desk to avoid an outright disturbance I finally did get the strap from Sister Mary Eva. Although I was a tad remorseful for putting myself in such a humiliating position before my peers, I was most fearful of my parents finding out because you know what that meant. Ouch yet again.

Many visits were made to the corner stores of both Glover's on Queen and Benny's right next to the school. My mom ran a tab at Glover's and many times I was sent to fetch a box of Cornflakes for her. As I arrived on the creaky wooden floor there sat a huge box wrapped in blue paper. I was then told to go right home as my mom would be needing them.

Numerous times I'd be taunted on the way home as my eyes barely saw over the top. "We know what's in the box. We know what's in the box." As I yelled out, "Cornflakes" somehow I felt I was being duped. I was later told I would learn all about it when I was twelve.

I particularly enjoyed stopping in at Benny's because of its proximity to the school. On Wednesdays we were always given coins for the Holy Childhood collection and I knew a few cents for penny candy would surely not be missed.

I loved going to school. It wasn't so much the learning as it was the socializing and it helped that I was good in sports so I always had a game to participate in at recess. And living across from the *big school* meant we knew pretty much everyone who went there. It was also comforting to be surrounded by so many others whose surname ended in a vowel so when it was time to give your father's name, uttering "Peo" drew very few looks. It was not uncommon to welcome new children each year just arriving from Italy. We all played a role in Canadianizing them.

You might remember periodic *turtle drills* at school when we'd all quietly march to the basement (where we would be safe) crouch on the floor on all fours and clasp our hands above our heads for maximum protection. And then there was the droning sound of the siren from St. David's Street. Not sure the intent but it was frightening to hear. This unspoken fear was supported in our own home where my dad built a bomb shelter in our basement which my mom would keep stocked with cans, boxes and bottles of nourishment … just in case.

Living so close to the border was a whole other perk. We immersed ourselves into the spirit of America by watching US TV shows and listening to *WKBW* radio. Deep down we secretly wished we were one of them.

We loved our monthly treks *over the river* which always promised some shopping for clothes never to be found locally; dinner at Como's; then perhaps the latest Doris Day movie. The ritual was always the same ... wear our oldest clothes over, rip the tags off the new ones and return home wearing them. They were always more appealing than the ones from the Eaton's catalogue and one notch more stylish than the clothing bought at McCall's in downtown St. Catharine's.

However our shopping buffet improved when we first heard the jingle: *"Come one come all to the Fairview Mall."* That was a huge event the day it opened as they lured us to the shops with an enticing array of amusement rides. But I still couldn't get my hands on a pair of those cool PF Flyers with the cushy soles just like the boys wore. No I had only a choice of Keds in white or black to choose from and it didn't help that the soles were virtually flat with no support. This soon became problematic for me as it appeared I was flat footed. My dad's remedy was to make me roll my feet on beer bottles to create an arch. It worked.

Rounding off our fabulous childhood in the sleepy town were weekend picnics at Port Dalhousie, occasional visits to Burgoyne Woods for a big outing and attending regular Bingo games in the church hall where my sole responsibility was to rip the red cardboard sheet into hundreds of little squares to serve as the markers. Special local treats included going to Riganelli's for a hunk of hand shaped bread, Avondale Dairy for ice cream, Henderson's Drug Store to weigh in (and hope no one was watching) then over to Steadman's for a walk around the aisles. Many Saturday afternoons were spent at the Tivoli to see the latest Three Stooges movie and still manage to get a treat with my twenty five cents.

One of my favourite places to visit in town was the Library where I wore out my card collecting every Bobbsey Twin, Nancy Drew, Cherry Ames and Hardy Boy book I could get my hands on. I'd read to and from school and manage not to step on one crack in the sidewalk the entire way. The only time I got distracted was in the winter when the huge hill in front of the Luciani (no relation) house on West Street beckoned my bum for a good slide. Years later on a return visit I was disappointed to discover it was merely a slight elevation. Wonder if the snow drifts were actually as high as I recall?

My worst memory of that stage in my life was the day the For Sale sign went up at 26 Whyte Avenue, a result of my dad being transferred. It was a frenetic day on the front lawn as we all took turns spitting at the sign in disgust at what it would mean to the friendships we had solidified with Ida, Josie, Cathy and the rest of the neighbourhood. The day we actually moved, 50 years ago, I remember that everyone was crying and hugging and promising to write. To downplay the significance of the event, I remember thinking that it really wasn't a big deal. It did not take me long to learn just how wrong I was.

Since then I have often wondered how my old friends and classmates have fared. Presumably most are aging well and successfully, yet sadly I am certain a few have already passed on. I can't drive past the Thorold exit without feeling nostalgic and rarely miss an opportunity to let people know that I proudly am from and still love Thorold.

Many have been quick to remind me that I would not have become the person I am today had we stayed in Thorold. But I have to disagree with them. I believe I am who I am today because of the early years (newborn to ten) I spent in Thorold. It was there I learned about fun and friendship, security and independence, adventure and acceptance. And for those life lessons I remain eternally grateful. Thank You.

Jugs

One morning, still flopping (literally) around in my pajamas, I was in the process of gathering the two large plastic, 18.5 litre water containers to drop at the front door, in hopes that someone would make an effort to have them filled.

As I neared the door I heard a light tap and saw through the bevelled glass that someone was standing there. So of course I answered the door still hugging a bottle under each arm.

There stood an police officer. Although my initial reaction was one of panic as I quickly accounted for each of my kids, the first words out of my mouth were not ones of concern.

Instead I foolishly uttered an invite into our home, "Please come in. And ah, excuse my jugs."

Thankfully the officer was female and had a sense of humour. She was quick to respond, "Which ones?"

I'm a Hoarder

The reality show *Hoarders* mystifies me. I really can't watch it for too long before I either want to be physically ill or reach that point when I yearn to don a mask, gloves and overalls and get in there and yell, "Outamyway, I'm coming in."

Now before you start thinking I live in a clutter-free, minimalistic environment, let me assure I don't. I confess I have stuff. Lots of stuff. But, I do value order.

I have old stuff with great emotional and nostalgic value; I have new stuff safely stored in my own version of Filene's Basement (the gift closet) and an entire collection of *you never know* stuff … as in you never know when it might come in handy. If you ever need a 1950's cash register, an entire set of old catcher's equipment or the Vic Tanney's vibrating exercise machine, let me know because I have it all resting comfortably amid a collection of similar treasures (sadly, to Joe it's junk).

But I believe I have a handle on my clutter. I purge regularly, make frequent trips to the donation bins and know everything I own and where it can be found. And besides, I live by the law: *what comes in must go out,* so there are limits.

Well that may be so in my home … but what about my head?

As I now prepare to enter the next age category on the survey sheet, the one that starts at 60, I realize I have to mentally declutter. I have reached my capacity to collect facts, figures and foolish fiction. I have exceeded the storage capacity for my brain and there's no going out and buying more RAM for it.

There really is no reason to hold onto the names of every

teacher I've ever had, the words to every Beatle song, latin conjugations or the other volumes of TUI (totally useless information) that I have been treasuring in my aging brain. And it doesn't help that I have been cursed with the ability to remember as far back as kindergarten, therefore I am the reference library for my oldest friends. Heck, no wonder I can't easily retrieve my kids' names or recall my own pins and cell number … I have clearly run out of room.

I must now determine what needs to stay and what needs to go. When something new and important enters my head then something old and stale must be released. If only there was an app for that, a delete button in our brain or a handle to flush away all of the vintage files. Then I'd be able to *phhtt, just let it go*.

So, I will do my best to put a stop to the hoarding in my head and continue to work on this cranial cleanse. And in the meantime please don't invite me to play Trivial Pursuit because I'll be trying to forget I know all of that stuff. And oh, if we happen to see one another, please do me a favour and introduce yourself and remind me of our past. If you'd like, make it up. I'll be too light-headed to notice.

Doctor … We Have to Talk

Hi my name is Carole and I just completed a self imposed two day cleanse as prescribed by you in *that* magazine. Dr., I readily admit I will try anything once, perhaps out of boredom; maybe for the challenge; often just to live to tell the tale. So I was intrigued that wintry day when I read about your 48 hours of *spring cleaning* where you promised the opportunity *to eat whole foods, nourish the body's detoxifying organs* and basically provide a good flush to the system of all the bad stuff.

I was intrigued not so much for me, but for my husband who, as a drug user (NOT that kind), surely must be filled with inner dust and particles needed to be cleared away. And since he is the family cook I would have to go along for the ride … and the challenge.

Here are my thoughts about the experience:

I was actually looking forward to it. I knew it had to be better than the Liquid Plumber, colonoscopy which not only flushes out every lingering morsel but leaves you tooting like a bread-wagon horse. I knew it wasn't about weight loss, although I would not turn my back (or side) to it. And you assured me I would not be left hungry. Thank goodness because it can get dangerous when that happens.

I took it upon myself to create a grocery list for Joe which was so extensive I thought of sending a search party out to look for him. He eventually did arrive home laden with enough bags of special ingredients to fill the entire counter. As I watched him unload, I studied the supplies, all foreign in our household … a whole load of '*c*' sounding foods like quinoa, cabbage, kale, caraway, cucumber and chia (all to be chopped) but not a carb in sight. I know it's Lent but c'mon where's the fun in that?

Without going through every step of your plan I will say other than my morning cuppa coffee, I followed it right through to your pointer about taking an evening bath with Epsom salts. Thanks to that suggestion it took me a good hour to make sure the tub was clean enough for me to bathe in, as it has been years since I indulged. I will admit however, the lounge time did give me an opportunity to plan our next bathroom renovation.

The breakfast was mediocre at best. Was the ginger and nutmeg really necessary? The between-meal snack was palatable but not tasty and way too green. The luncheon smoothie was actually pretty good except for the flaxseed lining my upper gums and teeth. And the dinner was well, somewhat nasty. I gotta tell you chewing on those shiitake caps reminded me of gnawing on my doll's rubber arm when I was a child. And the fermented sauerkraut chaser? Now I know that with all that vinegar, if there was a hint of a germ finding shelter in my digestive tract, it would be gone (lice despise vinegar, nail fungus shrivels up at the scent of it and weeds pass out and die when subjected to it). What starving gremlins designed this plan?

By dinner time I was giving Joe, the Vince Lombardi of life, the pep talk to not give up. Truthfully it's not that my attitude was much better, but I knew tomorrow was Day 2 and therefore, the last.

As you guaranteed there would be frequent trips to the washroom ... 14 on day 1, 16 on day 2 to be precise. I kept track. But that was just pee. I was so looking forward to *the other* of which I am generally most consistent with both frequency and constitution (sorry for sharing). I would ace your poop test. It didn't help that Joe had quickly boasted about his flush which was akin to the evacuation of a small village. By the 36th hour, I, on the other hand was CONSTIPATED!! I know what you're thinking that perhaps Joe was more full of s**t than me.

No fair. I eventually did have a few B.M.'s but nothing to brag about and certainly not worthy of the $100 grocery bill.

So, although you assured me I would physically feel better, I am left feeling gaseous and yearning for something explosive to happen to make it all go away. You mentioned it left you with a sense of peace ... funny, but not one person has said to me, "Oh, you look so calm, serene and peaceful." However my family has griped a few times about how grumpy I am.

And then you promised there would be a spiritual effect as well. Now you're right there because numerous times over the 48 hours I uttered our Lord's name in vain (mea culpa on that). But somehow I don't think that counts.

So in conclusion. I'm not happy. I experienced the two day cleanse and all I lost were two days of Joe's great cooking. Sorry but I must excuse myself ... I have some gas to pass.

P.S. While we're on the subject of B.M's, I must share a cute story I heard from a friend in Port Colbourne last weekend.

She had accompanied her Italian mother-in-law to the doctor's to act as an interpreter if needed. The serious doctor sat across from her, leaned in and asked in earnest: "Mrs. Spanelli, how are your bowel movements?"

To which she replied: "Che e balla movement? Me no hava no balls. Tony, he hasa da balls. Ana they no move."

The Valentine Fiasco

In January 1992, Joe and I were featured in a special pre-Valentine's Day article in the *Toronto Sun*. It profiled couples who *go the distance* in their relationship by doing special things for and with one another. At the end of the interview, the reporter asked me what exciting plans I had made for Valentine's Day this year. I just told her I was working on it.

What I finally decided on was a surprise for the whole family. I reserved a room at the Novotel in beautiful downtown Mississauga (okay, it doesn't matter where you go) and planned a little mystery tour that we could all enjoy. The children were two, five and seven. So it was that on the Friday in question, while many others were bathing for their evening date or rearranging the surprise roses in their vase, I was packing overnight bags for the five of us.

As soon as the boys arrived home from school we packed up the van and left for the hotel. I was pretty excited thinking about all the fun things we were going to do. Dinner, a movie, a walk around Square One, a swim in the pool. Yes, we could have fun anywhere we went. To make things a little less hectic, at the last minute I reluctantly arranged for my parents to watch Alena so Joe and I could have a chance to enjoy some time with the boys.

With everyone in high spirits we checked in and headed up to our room. I unpacked while Joe flopped in front of the television and the kids enjoyed a few quick tumbles off the bed. When I caught the boys eating from a bag of cookies that they had found under the bed, I realized that things would likely run smoother away from the room than in it. So I hustled them all out to go exploring at the mall.

The window-shopping thing lasted about twelve minutes and it's just not very relaxing to have to say NO so many times in a row. Since it was almost time for dinner we settled on a place right next to the theatre. The boys' behaviour started to deteriorate shortly after the meals had been ordered. Threats were delivered quicker than the food. Ignoring a popular parenting expert's advice to avoid threatening a consequence that is more punishment for you than the child, I didn't hesitate to start big: "Once more Vince, and you don't go to the movie."

Time to eat. I think it was the french fry up the nose trick that lost Vince any chance at popcorn that night. It was decided that Joe would take him back to the room as soon as the meal was finished.

I tried to enjoy my customary order of chicken caesar salad. Actually, it wasn't bad ... at least not until I pulled a twelve inch strand of blonde hair from between my teeth. I have always had zero tolerance for hair in places other than on one's head, especially when it belongs to someone else, so I made it a point to indignantly share my discovery with the waiter. Seeing that the blonde hair couldn't possibly have come from my own mane of inch and a half greys, he promised me a credit. My triumph was short-lived, however, as Dante proceeded to spill his drink all over himself and the table.

Checking the time, I hurried Dante along because the movie was scheduled to start in 10 minutes. We ran across to the theatre, only to encounter a long line up. By the time we reached the front of the line, I noticed that the time had been changed (I could not have possibly been wrong), and our movie had started 22 minutes earlier. Not a problem, we settled on another and it was okay.

When we arrived back at the room we saw that Vince had crashed in his clothes and it appeared that Joe had also enjoyed a wee bit of a snooze himself. Suddenly it hit me: Valentine's night with my family and Alena wasn't with us. It didn't feel right, so I urged Joe to go and get her from my parents. He hated the idea. It wasn't that it was far to drive, it's just that she was probably already nicely settled in her crib. But no, it just didn't feel right to me so he left to pick her up.

I quickly arranged for the crib to be set up, tightly jammed between the two double beds. I decided to fill the bathtub, knowing a warm soothing bath would feel great. I waited until it was at just the right depth, then stepped in to enjoy at least fifteen minutes of peace. Ready to lather up, I searched around for the soap. It was then that I noticed a slight ring below the waterline. Bubbles had built up along it. I traced it with my eyes and to my disgust, it travelled around the entire tub. I tentatively ran my finger over it to see if it was temporary. Yuck! I had been soaking in someone else's grime!

As I jumped up and out of the tub I saw Dante squirming into position on the toilet. It appeared he had saved everything for that moment. I encouraged him to finish up quickly. He flushed. Nothing happened. He pushed down on the metal handle again. Still nothing. The third try at least got it started, but it stalled halfway through, leaving us to watch the contents begin to float closer and closer to the rim. Pulllease! I realized I had to get someone from maintenance up there fast before the toilet actually overflowed.

Joe arrived back with Alena shortly after 10:00 p.m. He'd had to wake her from a sound sleep in order to bring her back to our hotel paradise. He was not pleased. She was ecstatic. I was fuming, still ticked about my interrupted bath and the malfunctioning toilet.

Joe and I tried to stay awake while we waited for the repairman to arrive. Dante finally crashed on one bed with Joe, who was still fully clothed, while Vince tossed and turned in the other. (Are couples actually supposed to sleep together on Valentine's Day?) Alena, in the meantime, was so wired that she was doing flips out of her crib onto the bed. At 1:20 a.m. she finally fell asleep. Dante was sprawled comfortably across Joe's body, so moving him was out of the question. There was still no sign of the repairman and I was totally exhausted, so

I put on my pajamas and settled in beside Vince. Tossing and turning like a mixed salad, I definitely did not rest that night. Whenever anyone dared go to the washroom, I screeched, "Don't flush that toilet!"

"Beep beep beep beep ..." What the heck was that? It took 15 seconds to realize it was the alarm clock. Somebody had set it for 5:00 a.m.! That was all we needed ... everyone woke up.

Bleary eyed, Joe and I desperately tried to keep the noise level down for any hotel guests who were enjoying a romantic stay, but as we watched the kids gleefully bounce around the room we knew it was a lost cause and decided to get dressed and go for breakfast. To make matters worse the toilet was only millimeters away from flooding the room. We quickly left the room and muzzled the kids all the way to the elevator.

It was now 5:30 a.m. and there we stood, a family of five in the hotel lobby. Couldn't go swimming ... too early. So, the kids huddled around the ledge and stared at the empty pool. Couldn't go to the dining room ... not open until 6:00 a.m. Joe nestled into one of the lobby chairs hoping for a quick nap. In a state of semi-craziness I decided it was time to talk to the manager on duty. Not one to let unmet expectations pass without comment, I approached the unsuspecting young person behind the counter and began my tirade.

I started with the opened bag of cookies under the bed. I continued with the unwelcome ring around the bathtub, followed by the overflowing toilet and missing repairman. The finale of course was the 5:00 a.m. alarm which, unfortunately for him, resulted in me standing at the front desk with nothing else to do but complain while I checked out.

The poor kid listened, nodded and tried not to wince. He expressed sympathetic disbelief and after extending a sincere apology on behalf of every possible department in the hotel, he politely asked, "Can I please have your room number, so I can look into this further for you?"

I dug for the key and handed it to the young man. With

an impish hint of humour he looked at the key and cheerfully joked, "Well this explains it!" The room number was 911.

While unpacking from our *vacation* at the ridiculous hour of 9:00 a.m., I found the other room key in my pocket. Knowing it would make a great souvenir I kept it and attached it to the carved heart Joe had already given me. It is a reminder of what will forever go down as the Valentine's night we'd love to forget.

The Gardening Casserole

*M*ost of us are at a loss for what to do to help someone in need. Regardless of their situation, we often feel helpless and wish we could in some small way ease their pain or sadness or merely lessen their load.

I discovered long ago that I was not going to be the one to knock on the door with Pyrex in hand delivering the familiar homemade-with-love-and-nutrition-casserole in their time of turmoil. Nope, that's not me. I don't cook, so that would be a major chore with less than satisfying results.

Fortunately though, I've learned that helping doesn't have to be restricted to the plate of food or even the card or flowers. And although the warm hug and compassionate ear are essential there are lots of other small acts that also provide comfort.

I have settled on gardening as my *casserole* of choice. I recognize that someone's surroundings typically reflect them, their current state of mind, body or soul. Often it's just lack of time that prohibits them from getting it done.

Entering their yard armed with time, talents and tools, the weeds get pulled, the plants get nurtured and the space gets restored and beautified.

This gesture is a satisfying one. I know it serves as much purpose as feeding their bellies or inspiring them with my words. It not only feels good to do something for a friend, but most importantly it enhances the beauty in their lives at that moment. It may not solve their problems but in a small way it does offer both calm and comfort to their situation.

So I challenge you to determine what your *casserole* is. When you do, give it away. The world will be thankful for it.

Don't Mean to Laugh ... But

*M*ost of us know better than to laugh at the misfortunes of others. It's not nice. As a humourist, I do my best to follow that code. I try to refrain from openly commenting about something I see involving someone less fortunate, whether related to physical ability, intelligence or appearance. Besides, I have often been on the other end so I understand the sting.

Nevertheless, I am not perfect. Situations do arise when squelching an outburst is a challenge. When events like this happen, they are usually memorable because it's often the incongruent qualities of a given situation that bring out the humour.

Recently, my friend and I went to the opening of a new shoe accessory store. It was the place to be with every trendsetter in town checking it out.

Immediately I knew there was no footwear on the shelves long enough to cover my feet, so I chose to wait by the entrance and people-watch.

I glanced from shopper to shopper, eavesdropping on their excited chatter. As I marvelled at the steady stream of eager bargain hunters, I noticed the security guard on duty by the doors.

He looked regal sitting there surveying the parade of people in his sight. He was clearly a senior and a big contrast to the typical uniformed staff you might see on duty *to serve and protect*. Adding to the oddity, there was a cane leaning up against his leg. Curious, I continued to watch him and noticed that he did not move without gripping the cane, not so much as a weapon but for support.

All I could think was, fat chance he'd be any threat to a fleeing shoplifter. Smiling, I created a cartoon in my head and envisioned myself dashing out, with him in pursuit. And as I fled, I'd turn back and taunt him with, "Nanny, nanny boo-boo. You can't catch me!"

Although I may not be the quickest on my feet, I was confident I could have certainly outrun the cane.

Nothing Beats A Bargain

It's gotta be genetic. I'm not sure what chromosome it is but it could very well be the dollar sign. It's the part of our DNA that sniffs out, searches for and ultimately spends on … anything. All in the effort to save money and be able to brag about it.

Such stories of $ucce$$ live on and are shared over and over to gasped responses of, "Oh my goodness", "I can't believe it" and inevitably "Oh that reminds me of the shirt I bought at Marshall's (or wherever else you choose to hunt bargains down)."

You have to admit it is fun even if you'll never use the 20 litre jar of maple syrup or consume the party pack of potpourri that you had to stop putting out because it looks edible and the kids kept reaching for it.

Joe once came home proudly hoisting a 25 pound bag of sugar purchased at the Price Club. To his disappointment I made him return it as I reminded him that based on our regular

consumption of sugar we would be collecting our pension before it was consumed. And besides we have no place to store it in our crowded little bungalow. It's just too easy to be overzealous with such super-sized offers.

But the real joy lies in both the hunt and the finish. The peak of exhilaration is achieved at the cash when the final amount is tallied after asking for a reduction because of the flaw, claiming your senior's discount status, using the coupon ripped from yesterday's paper and finally uttering, "What if I paid cash (an Italian favourite)?"

When my mom worked at Sears she never drew a wage because she received it all in purchased goods. It was a regular occurrence for her to return home laden with bags. She'd then dump each one while reciting the statement of savings to us which included all of the previously mentioned PLUS her employee discount. Finally one of us would drone, "Ma just tell us. How much did they pay you to take it?"

Admit it, we all have a great savings story. Some have too many to cite. Those are the super consumers who strategize their shopping excursions with a CAA highlighted map in hand indicating every outlet mall from here to Georgia with clipped coupons attached. My mother and sister fall into this category. They took our son Vince cross-border shopping from the time he was six months old to age 20 … only so that they could claim his *purchasing power* at the border. He increased their spending allowance considerably. Sadly, because of the annual experience, he too, possesses the shopping gene in size XL and in every colour.

Without mentioning names some will also use up $8 of gas to save $5 on a price match or will re-buy the identical item at the same price at a different location just to earn the extra 10 points. Let's face it … it's a game and some deserve to wear the champion's crown.

Another trait attributed to the super shopper is the one that will not allow acceptance of a compliment. Oh no. Someone casually says, "Is that a new shirt?"

Rather than simply saying, "Yes", it is quickly deflected by adding, "Oh it's the best story. We were shopping in Michigan at one of those outlet malls. We went into TJ MAXX and you know in the states how they're not afraid to mark it down until it's gone. WELL, it started out at $119.99 and by the time they rang it up it was $6.99. It's not the greatest fit for my body and it's not really a colour I should wear but heck you can't beat it. Besides if I only wear it a dozen times I can get it down to fifty cents a wear. It's like it's disposable."

OK so I might be one of those people. But let me tell you about the capri pants my friend Carol Ann just picked up for me at Sears. Great silvery grey colour. Nice sheen. Perfect pull up style with flattering wide waist band to hold the belly in. The best part is the stretch fabric. I was excited to receive them even if it was mid winter. As she handed them over she started her story. The *Coles Notes*: she paid $1.80. Her only regret was it wasn't *Super Sears Savings Day*.

Analyzing the drastic price reduction (typically foreign to retail stores in Canada) we figured it had to have been the sizing … 16 PETITE … clearly an oxymoron. Unless of course they're not capris at all but merely intended for shorter legs. It doesn't matter. I can't wait to wear them, and for someone to notice. Then gleefully share the story.

La Bella Figura

As an Italian I have been plagued by something I could not name for most of my young life. But finally in 1986, while visiting Joe's cousins in San Francisco, I was enlightened. It was then that, I discovered the affliction I was challenged by was known as *La Bella Figura*. Although the explanations about its meaning might vary, loosely translated it is *the good impression* … in other words: look and be your best at all times, in all places and with all people.

Conversely *La Brutta Figura* envelops all of your wrongdoings. That's a lot of polite-ical pressure, particularly for a young person.

I can't place all the blame on my mother. She merely inherited it from her mother. It's a traditional set of values passed down from generation to generation without anyone realizing it. I swear there exists a *Book of Proper* that never got translated. And I believe the essence of it is not about standing out but rather *not* standing out. In sharing this with friends, apparently it's not just the Italian culture that is ruled by such constraints.

Although I choose to live my life by the philosophy that I can do, say or wear anything I want as long as I am prepared to deal with the consequences, it has been an ongoing challenge. Here are just a few examples of the shackles I have struggled to free myself from since childhood:

"But I don't want to wear a dress. I'm not comfortable."

"You have to. Every other girl at the party will be wearing a dress and no daughter of mine will stick out by wearing slacks. Now just be a good girl and put the dress on."

*

"Did you get the invitation to the shower?"

"No and I hope I don't because I don't want to waste a perfectly good Sunday afternoon."

"Oh Carole don't talk like that. What if someone heard you?"

*

"You're going to the wedding aren't you?"

"No, I sent the reply back."

"But you'll send a gift right?"

"I wasn't going to. Why should I? I won't be there."

"It's only right. You don't want them to think you're cheap."

*

"Ah figlia, you better *make a visit* (funeral home). You don't want people to talk."

"Nona, who are these people you talk about? You never speak to anyone other than family. You rarely leave your apartment."

"Ah figlia … people, attsa it."

*

"Now why would you wear pink to the funeral home?"
"Ma, she was 95. It's a celebration."

"Oh I don't know. How's it going to look?"

*

"Tsk, Carole did you have to say that?"

"Oh Ma relax. I was just kidding."

"Well that wasn't nice. What if they thought you were serious? What will they think of you?"

*

"You're not going out wearing THAT are you?"

"Why? I like it."

"Well do what you want, I don't care. But I certainly wouldn't want to be seen looking like that."

CBL Code of Behaviour …
"I can do, say or wear anything I want … as long
as I am prepared to deal with the consequences"

*

And the *piece de resistance* :

"Carole, can't you just try to be normal?"

"But Ma, it's just not as much fun."

I continue to deal with the fallout of my miscues. In defense of my mother or her fore-mothers, I admit I have been heard to say to my own children, "Can you please not draw negative attention to yourself?" The message rings of familiarity. At least I come by it honestly.

P.S. C'mon please admit it that you too struggle with similar passages from the imaginary *Book of Proper*. You do, don't you? Please tell me. It will make me feel so much better.

Not Seeing Eye to Eye

Ever notice how some of your best attempts at humour are lost because the other person is either not paying attention or is so riddled with tension it just does not compute?

I was having a smudge on my eyeball looked at and there I stood within nose whiskers of the specialist. Instrument in hand, magnifying the blob, he confirmed in muffled tone, "It's nothing more than an ebulia."

Remaining still, in my position opposite him, I calmly blew back onto his face, "Is an ebulia an annual or a perennial?"

He immediately retracted the instrument stepped back and sternly announced, "I'll send the report to your family doctor."

Huh. The mild attempt to introduce some levity into the interaction could have made his day … but he just couldn't see it.

The Dickey

Thank you to the inventor of the dickey and for introducing it to the world of fashion (circa 19th century). My first exposure to it was in the mid 1960's when my entire wardrobe could easily have fit into the smaller sized suitcase of the three-piece set. With the availability of this new $2.99 accessory I could multiply my fashion options tenfold without having to pay for the torso and sleeves.

Suddenly, with the availability of this fabric collar insert, I was able to add variety to my wardrobe. And since there was little upper body pawing or probing going on, no one recognized it as a facade from the distance.

It provided multiple benefits combining both illusion and insulation and was clearly an enhancement to my overall look. After all, most agree that something worn up to the chin is uplifting. As well, it possessed the ultimate *cool* factor as it hugged my tortoise length neck. And when worn in black it not only aligned me with the beatnik crowd but also made my neck look slimmer (that is a fashion fact is it not?). Most helpful was the authentic *one size fits all* label, unlike so many of the other pieces of clothing that definitely that falsely made the same claim.

Beyond the assorted cotton selection available in most retail fashion accessory departments my knitting aunt was resourceful enough to replicate it in various hues of cozy wool so my neck was never to be exposed or shivering. I had an entire pallet to choose from each day to complete my duffle coat outerwear look. Aside from potentially disturbing the hairdo, it was a quick fix to the blank canvas of any open, bare and boring neckline.

So it's nice to see the rebirth of the dickey now available in 172 looks of varying style, fabric and colour. I just hope they've been smart enough to introduce some adequate stretch from the esteemed Lycra family. This of course would only appeal to those of us who actually wore them over 40 years ago. The only problem with the added stretch is that the fat it would squeeze out of position would have to go somewhere else … and hopefully not to our face or chest. Maybe I can redirect the now loosely hanging flesh to meet at the nape of my neck and then nicely drape a scarf. Or then again it just might inspire the rebirth of the mullet for adequate camouflage.

My Social Media Card's Full

*H*elp!! This world of online socializing is making my head spin. I can't seem to find the time to meet with my *real* friends in person I'm so busy playing nice with strangers.

It started innocently enough. My friend Linda urged me to join *Facebook* claiming I was a natural for it. I reluctantly welcomed it into my life. Before I knew it I was being asked to be a friend … I don't remember being asked that since playing in the Holy Rosary school yard in the 1950's. Quickly my list grew. It helps to be related to lots of people with surnames ending in an vowel. Besides it's bad manners to say NO.

Facebook proved to be an invaluable tool not to mention time waster. It allowed me to play Scrabble without having to invite someone over, look at photos of how my kids spent their weekend, and find out that a relative has separated. ("But Ma, it's true. They just changed their *status*.") I played nicely, commented on most, clicked *like* to postings 'n pics and slowly emerged into a regular *poster* without ever bragging about what I ate for dinner or that I just hit the jackpot on the game, Roll the Dice.

I was soon meeting with my web specialist, Jemma who casually mentioned that as a writer (Really? I'm going to track down my university prof who gave me an F + in The Use and the Abuse of the English Language), I should consider blogging as a means to show people my stuff. So I did. And I continue to do so with now close to 200 posted. At least I know my six close friends are reading them.

Then someone wagged her finger at me and uttered the commanding words, "You really need to hook up with *LinkedIn*." Obediently, I did. After a brief period of time, however, I discovered my profile showed my landscape business in prominence with little attention to my speaking career. This led to being introduced to a large audience at a conference as the Chief Weed Whacker and Master Edger of Yard Duty with no mention of my role or experience as a speaker. I had a lot of explaining to do.

My kids soon started nattering, "Mom, you would be an awesome tweeter. You gotta tweet. Mom, it would be great for your business." As I learned more about it, I realized it's merely a chance to stick our tongues out at that childhood law: *we must be seen but not heard* which no longer applies. It's just one incessant string of chatter and no one has to show their face. *Twitter* is like yelling into the wind ... a whole lot of talk but is there any real listening going on? Please convince me.

Sitting in silence (yes I can sit in silence), I pictured the hanging in my kitchen of *Birds On A Wire*. I imagined the scene of one bird telling another who turned and told another who told his twirp club, who then announced it at early morning worm picking, who then shared it with her entire extended family and so on and so on and ...

I soon joined the *party line*. However once I mastered the terminology (tweeting not twittering or as my mom calls it, *doing the twitter)* I seemed to attract rap artists, street wear fashionistas and African American talent agents. It seems I got their attention after I tweeted asking if I could try out for a role in the all black version of *Steel Magnolias.*

I knew I was lagging behind so I succumbed and attended a seminar with social media medic, Amy. Through her urging I was soon hooked up with *Hoot Suite, Stumble Upon, Ezine Articles and Digg* … I was barely breathing at this point being pounded by a plethora of posts, profiles and passwords (now that was an awesome alliteration). Truthfully I have since fallen off many of those wagons.

Next came a re-introduction to *YouTube* and the directive that I must start posting more videos of myself and my work. Thus the presentation of my CBL Vintage Video Series. No boasting intended but I'm pretty certain my audience is well over six viewers per video at this point. Please don't tell anyone as I would hate for it to crash from over exposure or perhaps catch that viral bug.

Recently I attended another social media presentation by guru Lisa at a women's weekend. With her insistence I checked into *Klout* … just to see if I had any. Apparently nowadays when someone asks about your numbers it has little to do with how many you may have slept with. Surprisingly my score was a whopping 35 … not bed-mates but my Klout score.

Then by slowly paying some attention to it, apparently I became a *specialist* and before I knew it, my influence and Klout score climbed to a whopping 50. Oddly though it seems that I have a lot of clout in Family, Comedy and wait for it …. the Circus. Huh, who knew? I guess they've seen those photos of me wearing the red nose in the Oakville Santa Claus Parade or maybe have heard my family whine about being sent to Circus School when they were kids. But comedy? Not if my kids had anything to say about it.

At that same women's weekend, I spent some time with Elaine, another aficionado of the social media world. Her pitch … "You HAVE TO be part of *Google* +." Not knowing whether it might be another example of super sizing or possibly a group for those of us who are over size 12, I made a mental note to look into it.

Shortly, an online chat with her began. She shared her expertise, time and patience and I was guided through the set- up portion. Unfortunately *hanging out* on Google + requires full make-up, a lifted jaw (to avoid that drooping beagle look) and to avoid scaring others out entirely ... sitting an adequate distance back from the webcam. Perhaps those apps available to enhance your image (like the pirate headgear or moustache - no, wait I think I have that covered) just might be useful after all.

So here I sit with no time to get dressed let alone clean my house or do any work for pay. I need a haircut, manicure, pedicure and a complete body sugaring but there's just no time. Please dear Lord don't have anyone invite me to *hangout*. They might find my billy goat look disturbing.

Sadly, my time is currently consumed with making new friends (shh don't tell my old friends, they'll be upset with me) with complete strangers from all over the continent. Who knows what aspect of my profile they might be picking up on enticing them to befriend me but it's happening. Surely, the circus crowd can't be far behind.

Good Grief

*A*fter graduating from University I had the opportunity to travel across Canada with my friend Nancy. With a limited budget we scheduled our numerous stops to include overnight visits with friends and relatives along the route … which satisfied considerably more than economics.

Arriving in Vancouver we were fortunate to be able to stay with Nancy's Aunt Mary and Uncle Bill. They invited us to enjoy their home as the west coast base for both our day trips and overnight excursions. They eagerly welcomed us with open arms and a place setting for every meal, complete with our own linen napkin. They were very hospitable and extremely entertaining which made it easy for us to relax and contribute to the rhythm of their home. We finished each evening off with a night cap and a round of stories.

Nancy and I shared a room with two single beds, still set up with furnishings from the time their own children lived there. We'd yak and giggle ourselves to sleep and then cheerfully awaken each morning to Aunt Mary's gentle tap on the door to tell us that breakfast was ready.

Early one morning, we heard the familiar tap and Aunt Mary opened the door just a crack. In the same warm and gentle pre-breakfast voice, she announced, "Good morning girls. I'm sorry to tell you Uncle Bill passed quietly in the night." And then with little hesitation, she added, "Breakfast will be served whenever you're ready."

We were stunned by the news. We had no response as it came as such a shock to us. We were speechless, not just because of the suddenness of his death but by the casual nature of the delivery of the news.

As I stared across the floor to Nancy, I shot her strong non-verbal signals begging for an explanation. Growing up Italian, such restraint and stoicism were not behaviors I recognized and attributed to mourning. Even Nancy was surprised by the matter of fact manner in which we were informed.

What followed was equally foreign to me. There was no drama about the occurrence; no details were shared of the late night event and definitely no tears were openly shed. Wow. I could not believe what I was witnessing. His surprise *passing* fell into place with the regular routine of the night and with little interruption to our day. It was as though he had slipped out quietly, careful not to slam the door and wake us from our sleep. After all, we were guests in his home.

The next few days were very enlightening to me. I tried to stay out of the way of the influx of friends and relatives arriving from all over the country. And as I remained in the background I did pay attention to the open acceptance of his *death from natural cause*s as well as the celebration of his life, albeit a shortened one.

I enjoyed Uncle Bill in the brief time I was with him. He was fun, warm and engaging. He was definitely loved and would be missed by those who knew him.

In time, I was able to appreciate the calm, quiet and gentle acceptance of death as an alternative experience in mourning style I was accustomed to. I learned through the experience that although there appeared to be little sorrowful emotion shown, it was in no way indicative of the feelings people had for him. The displays of grief and sadness differed but were no less sincere or meaningful.

She Never Noticed My Hair

I am regularly jolted by assumptions that other adults, who are often older than me, make about my age. They think that just because my hair is white, it has to mean I'm older than I am … and them. It stings. Admittedly it's a hang-up I'm trying really hard to accept.

. A few years ago I enjoyed a weekly volunteer stint in my friend Lori's kindergarten class, where I was known as Mrs. B. I loved the kids and being with them drew out the aging kid in me.

On occasion a few of the children said things that led me to believe they looked at me like their grandma, but I excused them for it … they were four years old. Besides, I *was* old enough to be their grandma.

One day after my morning visit, I went into the office to sign out. As I stood at the counter, a child from the class entered with her mother. I overheard her whisper, "Mom, see the girl with the red top. That's Mrs. B."

Her innocent comment diminished every wrong assumption previously made by adults. Thank you Sarah. You made my day.

On the Face of Time

The other day while I was working at my desk, I caught my reflection. I was disturbed by what I saw ... not just because I am now living proof of the modified verse: *"Mirror, mirror on the wall ... yikes, I've become my mother after all."* But no, it was more than that.

I looked closely and was shocked by the natural downturn of my mouth. Hmm, I immediately checked my current state of mind and affairs ... kids were all accounted for, husband

was still there, just spoke with my mom and at that moment I was physically feeling pretty good. In a quick summation there was nothing deserving of such a downcast expression. Sadly, as I then glanced at my watch, I saw grave familiarity. The hands showed 8:20 ... it was a mirror image of my mouth.

Pondering this for a moment, I knew I had a long way to go to achieve an 11:05 (as suggested by my friend, Dian); intense focus would be required for even a 10:10; and heck even a flat liner look of 3:45 would necessitate some muscle (literally, as I believe it is the risus muscle). As I thought about the seriousness of this issue I realized that shockingly, perhaps my passport photo IS the real me. I was so fraught with despair that I quickly jumped up to scan old family pics only to make the sad discovery: "Oh my ... it's GENETIC."

Now the lesson here is that my ancestors were not naturally miserable people ... they just looked like they were (that photo  was taken at a wedding ... can you imagine their funeral faces?). It takes no real energy at all to go through life and look like that. Try it. It's easy and effortless and you can slowly grasp the permanent mood this beholder must enjoy ... or not. And it wouldn't take long until you get really comfortable with *the feel,* much like your favourite jeans or loafers. And before you know it, there is some permanence to *the look.*

Unfortunately there are no inherent benefits to this expression.

The laborious effort takes place when we want to change *the look.* We do it for posed photos all the time. Here's a tip: Forget saying, "Cheese." It leaves your mouth way too tight. Try mouthing, "Thursday" instead. Quick, go check yourself in the mirror. It works. For a split second anyway.

So I now have a better understanding of the people who go through life with the grave expression of *doom 'n gloom* plastered on their face. They are the flat liners. They can't help it that they look like that but they can help try to change it. Sadly it will require some time and energy. And truthfully, most have already convinced themselves they have neither of these.

Fortunately I have been blessed with loads of both so I'll keep trudging along trying to make the best of what life and heredity offer, even if it hurts my resting risus muscles. I know it's worth it.

Something Good is Gonna Happen

I can't remember exactly when it bloomed but there is strong evidence that the optimism seed is flourishing in the base of my brain. Its blossom affects most everything I do, casting rose coloured hues to obscure my vision. Its aroma is so strong I can't ignore it. It affects most thoughts floating freely out of my head. And it is downright laughable.

I won't buy lottery tickets when the pot is high because I believe winning will ruin my life; as I prepare to tee off on a par 3, I wonder how much it will cost me to buy a round after the 'hole-in-one' I am about to score; and after sending out an unsolicited book to a magazine editor for review I wonder how I will deliver the hordes of boxes they will inevitably want.

I know it's crazy but I assume I will win the door prize, am certain that Oprah will eventually accept my email invite to come for dinner and am confident that my kids will one day *get* all the stuff I've been harping about over the years. (Oddly the optimism doesn't interfere in with my ability as an Italian mother to worry about all things concerning my kids.)

Interestingly rather than be continually disappointed with the *no show* of the desired outcome, I somehow find that the ever present hopeful thoughts make me laugh out loud. And for that I am thankful. I can be heard woefully sighing my mantra of choice: "Something good's gonna happen." It also serves as my reminder to shake it off, let it go and move on.

I guess it's because I want to believe it will. And in doing so, I will continue with my rosy outlook because it sure beats the doom of the alternative. Besides, it keeps me alert and on guard for the *good*. I'd hate to miss it when it does show up.

Chug-a-lug

One of the things I learned quickly and practised often when I entered university was how to drink beer. Draft was my drink of choice and it helped that it cost only ten cents a glass at the Kent Hotel. My friends and I usually drank Thursday, Friday and Saturday nights and any other time the offer came up. The newly acquired habit contributed to both the loss of my academic standing and the gain of my girth, but we really did enjoy this recreational pursuit. We especially loved it when the song *American Pie* was blasted over the speakers in the pub because it was our signal to jump onto the chairs and belt out the lyrics in unison.

Midway through the first semester, a flyer was posted on campus, which advertised an event that had our names written all over it. The student union was hosting the inaugural BOAT RACE CHAMPIONSHIP for any interested teams of recreational drinkers. Well, that's all we needed to clear our calendars and start training in earnest.

The requirements entailed entering a team of four drinkers with one sub to fill in if needed. The competition would pit one team against another in a relay-type contest. Looking around our East B dorm, it was easy to field our team.

The rules of play were simple. Full glasses of draft were placed along a table and the team would be asked to step forward and take their spots. At the sound of the bell, the first drinker would bring the glass of beer to her mouth, chug it back, slam the empty vessel on the table, hoist it back over her right shoulder and once again slam it down to signal her completion and for the next drinker in line to proceed. The team that finished first moved along in the tournament draw and was required to continue drinking in the rounds that followed. It's a good thing we had practised.

Round one went without a hitch and we earned the win. Round two took place after drinking lots of water and again we were victorious. Round three was a close one but we prevailed and managed to move on. By round four, we were feeling the effects of the low percentage alcohol.

Our spirits were buoyed by the possibility of going all the way. What an achievement that would be. With shower caps on our heads and excited to take on those boozers from the other dorm, we were oblivious to the crowd of spectators that had gathered in the pub.

Ding! The round began. First drinker cleared; second drinker cleared; third drinker was JP and as she slammed the glass for the first 'down', it broke. Continuing on sheer adrenalin, she hoisted the broken glass once again but it got away from her shoulder and met with the flesh beneath Mary Ann's left eye. Not missing a beat, she continued with lightening speed, earning us another victory and a pass into the finals.

It wasn't apparent to any of us what had just happened to Mary Ann, but as we celebrated we saw the blood gushing from her face. Treatment was available immediately and she was whisked off for stitches. In our scrambled (i.e. drunk) thinking we were very thankful ... that we had a sub to replace her.

The final round was set. The teams were introduced and the bell was rung for the last time that night. It was nearing midnight and although we were close to saturation, we were pumped to compete for the championship and bragging rights. The details of the next round were much like the previous ones so all I need to say is WE WON!!

Hugging, cheering and more beer drinking ensued in celebration of the athletic feat that had just taken place. We were ecstatic about the win and incredibly proud to hoist the engraved pewter mug we had earned. Heading back to the safety of our dorm for more celebration, all I could think of was the importance of sharing this momentous occasion with my family.

Ignoring the time on the clock, which I could barely read anyway, I called home. I was certain my parents would be elated. They were always big supporters of our athletic achievements, especially my dad.

It rang six times before my father answered (in those days there was one phone, downstairs in the kitchen). Bypassing the usual pleasantries, I blurted out, "We won! We won the boat races!"

"What the hell is a boat race?"

"Beer chugging. Our team won the campus beer chugging contest and I was on the team. That's what all the noise is about in the background."

I knew that my father was never one to hide his feelings or mince his words, but I was certain he hadn't understood my good news because the yelling on the other end of the phone was starting to hurt my head. All I really remember from the one-sided conversation that followed is this.

"G** Damn it to hell. Is that the G** Damn reason I sent you to university? Is that where my hard-earned money is going? You phoned to wake us up to tell us that? JC almighty, if you were here right now ...."

He just didn't understand.

On Time's Too Late

I had arranged to take my mother out one day to a few appointments. As I was about to leave my house I called her to let her know what time I'd be there so that she could be ready.

"Ma I'm just leaving the house now so I'll be there in 15 minutes to pick you up. That'll give us enough time to be in Hamilton for 10:00."

She was quick to reply, "Oh I'm glad you called. I was just going to phone you. Any chance you can leave 10 minutes earlier? I'd like to stop at The Bay first."

I Resolve to ...

*E*ntering this new year like everyone else I have taken my first step in my journey from fat to fit (I have a pet name for myself that my friends know but I will not share due to its profanity). So here are my back-to-the-gym resolutions ...

1. I will not be caught dead wearing a baseball cap while I work-out indoors ... because if I did I should also wear sunscreen and sunglasses. I deem all of these to be completely unnecessary and a breech of suitable dress code for the indoors.

2. I will refrain from feeling compelled to show more flesh in my workout attire ... if I felt fit enough to show more flesh I wouldn't feel the need to work-out, hence I will stay with my long pants and sleeves.

3. I will hold back from the urge to prove to the rest of the gym that I too have both the resources and style to wear 'lulugear' ... since the only thing that fits me from their selection is the headband and I doubt that would impress anyone as it just makes my hair stick out and up even more.

4. I will restrain myself from listening in on the loud chatter around me, particularly those personal conversations of intimacy shared in tones for all to hear ... it's not that I don't want to but my unsolicited comments are not always appreciated or welcomed.

5. I will prevent myself from prolonged gawks below the waist, front and back at the guys around me ... my husband made me promise.

6. I will stop myself from judging those fitness obsessed calo-

rie deprived fanatics ... God bless them ... I dare not tell them a good laugh could be exercise enough.

7. I will do everything in my power to resist the urge to say something to that bitch scowling back at me through the mirror as I stretch, push and bend my body ... oops that person is me.

8. I will resist sneaking peaks at the person and machine next to me secretly believing with great certainty I could work at that level too ... it's just that I'd rather not ... not today anyway.

9. I promise to go from doing squat to doing squats and from exercising my right to rant and rave to just plain exercising. And I will acknowledge that standing over a machine and talking to someone for 15 minutes does not count in my one hour work-out.

10. I will do my very best to work-out like a horse ... after all they are supposedly the only ones who sweat.

P.S. If my efforts at the gym are not successful I will continue to run off at the mouth, jump to conclusions and stretch myself to the limit. That's exercise enough for me.

Can't See for Lookin'

*Y*ears ago, we joined five families for a March Break trip to Myrtle Beach. Each day the moms headed to the beach for a walk and a yak. We covered a lot of ground … in subject matter. Babbi and Rita each toted their heavy cameras determined to snap photos along the route. When we returned with the cameras invariably untouched, they would unwaveringly declare, "Tomorrow we have to get a picture."

Each day the temperature increased as did the number of people on the beach By our final day, the sandy strip was packed with bathers, players and walkers. And we had yet to capture or pose for a single picture.

Determined to pop the lens cover at least once for the souvenir shot, Rita finally announced, "OK, that's it. I've got to ask someone to take our picture." She stopped, looked around and with me in tow, approached an older woman standing nearby. "Excuse me. Would you mind taking our picture?"

The woman turned and directed her wrap-around green glasses somewhere between the two of us and replied, "Oh I'm sorry dear, but I'm blind."

Embarrassed by our error, we sincerely apologized and turned to walk in silence. But it was a struggle in self control as the bubbles of laughter billowed from our bellies. With 2,000 people on the beach that day, how was it we managed to find the one woman who was unable to see? We only hoped when she returned to her family on the beach, she would be amused enough to say, "Let me tell you what just happened …"

Catch A Mood Lately?

*G*erms are everywhere. We catch a cold, catch the flu or the latest virus. But rarely do we read about or talk about the effects of catching a mood.

Imagine a good day. You have a tickle on your heart, a sparkle in your eye and a smile on your face. You're happy to be alive and excited to share your good humour with the world.

But, wait. There's someone out there with another agenda. *Misery is her mission* and *pity is her passion*. Upon meeting Mona (Miserable Mona for short), you innocently ask a simple question: "How are you doing?"

Whoa. It appears Mona has been waiting months for someone to personally acknowledge her existence.

"You wanna know how I'm doing? You wanna know what it's like to be pre - peri - menopausal as each of my kids are going through puberty? You wanna know what it's like to retain the swells of lake Ontario in my joints with every step? You wanna know what it's like to tell your son it's time to shave and he says "I'll start when you do?""

Mona's on a roll.

You are not prepared for her whiny outpouring. Her *woe is me* monologue is in the long version when all you wanted was the abbreviated form. As an upbeat and optimistic individual, ordinarily you would quickly interject, "Now Mona let's sprinkle a little joy on this conversation."

But it's too late for that. The tone has been set at *doom 'n gloom* and you don't have time to prepare your defences.

You're completely caught off guard. You listen intently to

everything she has to say. You nod with compassion as you lean closer to hear everything that is being said without interference. Your eyes are firmly focussed on hers. And as you listen, a strange thing happens. Seemingly a dark cloth has been draped over you obscuring your vision. It weighs heavily on your heart. Suddenly the view around you has been reduced to one very narrow dark tunnel.

Mona's drone continues ...

Her dog's on medication. He can't sleep alone anymore since eating the Ikea furniture. Their basement flooded when they were away visiting her sick father-in-law who was just recently placed in a home. Their youngest has lice and she's fearful the other kids will get them too. Her husband's job is not as secure as he'd like and to top it off she's having more of those hot flashes.

You stop to check yourself. The smile has left your face. The weight of your plumped cheeks now droops heavily over your mouth. Your body has slackened into a hunched position. You are now a mirror image of Mona. You have been zapped by her toxic contagion and you have lost control of your own positivity.

Mona's secret desire came true. She has successfully de-moodivated you. Every ounce of energy, every splash of endorphins (those good feelings we get from being upbeat, joyful and positive) and every pleasant thought that ever filtered through your mind has been deleted ... gone to the verve vacuum deep within your spirit.

Now there are two of you feeling low-ful and woeful. Before long there will be four ... and so on and so on and so on .

Put an end to the downward spin cycle at once. *Moodivate* yourself before someone *de-moodivates* you. And if you need some assistance with that ... contact me.

I Love My Garage

My earliest memory of a garage was the one my dad built. It sat back and away from our small bungalow in Thorold. Along the side of it was a garden and nestled behind was our metal swing set where we played until our heads spun.

The inside of the garage was cold and dark. It was a haven for spiders and other moving things so I didn't spend much time in there other than to quickly retrieve a bike, shovel or tool for my dad. I really don't remember there being anything else even in there. Since there was no electricity it was always difficult to find what we needed unless it was daylight. Besides, it was the carport leading up to it that got the most use.

But it seemed our neighbours in Thorold found other uses for their garages. Many had tables and chairs set up; some full kitchens with appliances; some made their wine in there; and many had carpeting. It was not uncommon on a nice summer day to see them sitting side by side, in or just outside their garage with a drink in hand, watching the world go by (this usually took place after watering their driveway). It was their outdoor all-weather rec room, offering more supplies and protection than the veranda.

I didn't acquire my own single-sized garage until ten years ago when we renovated. I couldn't wait for storage space for our once openly displayed collection of stuff. Looking inside it now I wonder how we managed to maintain any hint of *curb appeal* with just the carport.

What else are we to do with space other than fill it? I now have it organized with curb-side discarded shelving, curtains and a peg board system for my gardening tools and an eclectic assortment of bins and hooks. Currently it is packed. Seasonal equipment and accessories, furnishings and stray pieces of junk collected but banned from the interior of our residence now rest there comfortably. It's home to bikes, skis, building material and more. But it is orderly. I know where everything is, it all has a use and I joyfully rearrange it all weekly. And I too now have some carpeting to cushion the cold of the concrete.

Since my garage never came with a user guide, I was unaware that some actually use it as a place to park their car. My neighbour once issued a challenge to see if I could even fit a car in there. I achieved the goal, but he never did pay up with case of Stella. Perhaps it was because although I could drive the car in ... I could not open the door to get out.

Yes, I openly admit, "I love my garage", not as much as my bed but definitely as much as Joe loves the kitchen. Could it be the lowered levels of estrogen and increased levels of testosterone (or vice versa) we are experiencing? Who knows, but I think I'll head outside right now to organize it once again. Then I might grab a chair and a drink and watch the world go by ... but I won't water the driveway until tonight when it's dark. I'd hate for someone to see me.

Lucky Ducks

Friday afternoon rush hour in six lanes of Waterloo traffic and suddenly our car and every other around us came to an obedient halt.

There, directly in front of us was a family of ducks, four baby chicks no taller than five inch trailed by a squawking mommy urging, coaxing and encouraging each of them from behind. She dare not look to her sides as she was intent on getting her family safely across the street all the while probably wondering "What was I thinking? I should have at least waited to cross at the light."

As they hurried (the most hurried one can get with webbed feet and a short four inch stride) across the pavement, there was not a hint of complaining; no stopping to plea for a pick-up; nor any whines of, "Are we there yet?" or "My webbed feet really hurt."

Yep, that mommy did what all of us would do … stay focused on the mission and keep moving like you mean business because no one's gonna mess with my babies.

And, as we waited in our idling cars, we didn't. And those lucky little ducks made it safely across those six lanes without a screech of a tire, a toot of a horn or a threat of making it onto someone's plate for dinner.

P.S. It was clear the mommy duck had instilled a positive attitude in her chicks … "You can do anything if you just keep moving forward."

Uncle Gino's Trunk

My mother had a cousin we called Uncle Gino. Although he grew up in Hamilton, he spent most of his adult life in New York City owning a bowling alley and living in Queen's. He never married so every child from our multi-branched family tree became his own to spoil. And he provided for all of us.

Uncle Gino was a bargain hunter, a deal maker and a collector, all of which he did with a generous spirit.

We were the only family at the time to leave Hamilton, settling in Thorold, close to the US border. This proved to be beneficial as we were the first stop of many on his frequent trips home.

It didn't matter where we were playing because once the word got out that the long, dark Lincoln with the US plates arrived on Whyte Avenue, we dropped everything to greet him and welcome him back.

It wasn't only his loving and affable nature that endeared him to us. It was also what was in his trunk. After pulling into the driveway, the first thing he did was extend his arms out for hugs. Then he'd pop open his coveted car trunk to both display and distribute his most recent acquisitions. We didn't question our good fortune, we just knew there were treasures somewhere buried within the stash and we eagerly awaited 'the shopping' within. To us it was Christmas in July.

Uncle Gino's nose for bargains was not without an eye for trends as he amassed heaps of shoes, clothing and accessories not yet appearing in the stores of our little town. This allowed us to break away from the popular Eaton's catalog styles commonly worn by everyone else. We wore bleeding madras before our friends knew the phrase, slop hats and short sleeved sweatshirts with TK jeans when not in our school uniform; and coloured Keds not yet available in Canada. Selected pieces were ours for the picking as long as we left enough for the rest of our cousins in Hamilton. We were so appreciative that it was common for all of us to trade or hand-around (as opposed to hand-me-down) the items to the rest of the extended family as we outgrew them.

As well, his visit was not complete without presenting each of us with a specially chosen item. How he knew our likes and interests one will never know. And with every treat we were granted from his trunk he had a story to share in his acquired New York accent. We loved every moment spent in his company.

Now years after his death, rarely do any of we cousins meet without sharing our own Uncle Gino stories. We not only expound on his warmth, humour and generosity we so fondly remember but can also easily recall our most prized possession retrieved from the back of his car.

For me it is my coveted four fingered leather Rawlings baseball glove given to me in time for my Bird League debut in 1960. It remains prominently displayed in my home as my reminder of Uncle Gino's legendary trunk.

Residential Revelations

I have always maintained a huge costume box loaded with goodies collected over the years. It has served as the *go to* source for numerous costume parties, Hallowe'ens and parades.

One year I hit a clearance sale and snagged some key pieces for the stash. One coveted item was a red negligee trimmed with a red boa fringe. I knew it would be a welcomed addition to the other odd pieces that sat in the trunk.

When Alena was around four, like many little girls she enjoyed dressing up. One of her favourite get ups included a bikini, a pair of hand painted cowboy boots, a sequined ball cap and the beloved red, baby doll length negligee. She loved that outfit. Mardi Gras or not, she paraded up and down our quiet street, sometimes riding her bike and sometimes dragging her furry friends in the noisy wagon. Being the only little girl on the street, she got a lot of attention.

Years later as we were enjoying a block party with our neighbours, someone started reminiscing about the kids and how fondly she remembered Alena and her antics. "I'll never forget her wearing that outfit of hers … the bikini, those oversized cowboy boots and the best was YOUR red negligee."

Before I even had a chance to dispel the misinformation about the true ownership of the negligee, the others jumped in to concur. They especially enjoyed the image of me in the negligee and asked if I had the slippers to match. Apparently they looked at me differently after seeing that negligee.

I was horrified. It took me some time but I managed to assure them it was NOT MY negligee and that my sleepwear of choice at the time was a pair of cotton cowboy pajamas.

To this day, I'm not convinced they believed me.

It's Best Done in Private

The earliest memory I have of flatulence (I know it might offend some of you) has to do with my father. At the time, I figured it was just something that he did, but then I heard a similar sound from my brother and assumed it was a guy thing.

A short time later though, when Nona was taking a bath I heard a terrific rumble emerge from the bathroom that sounded like something had ricocheted off the sides of the tub. I called out to her, "Nona, are you okay?"

I can still hear her laughing. "Ah figlia, I had to blow. You know it's not so good to keep it in."

This challenged my theory about flatulence being exclusive to men, and I began thinking that perhaps it was an Italian thing.

I believe I was in the first grade when one day in class I heard, smelled and felt something that was both foul and faintly familiar to me. I looked around and there, smugly holding in a laugh, was Donny B. That solidified my new theory, because he himself had way too many vowels in his last name.

My world expanded soon after when one day, in that same class, someone from behind *let one go*. As it crawled up my back and into my space, I knew, hands down, no question, there was a flaw with the saying: *those who smelt it dealt it*. It was absolutely obvious who had to claim ownership. And that was the boy sitting right behind me. Deon (the name has been changed to protect the guilty) was the one. Not so much offended by his inappropriate act but rather shocked about his heritage, I remember turning around and holding my nose, uttering, "Psst … Deon. I didn't know your were Italian."

He gave me a quizzical look. "Huh? What are you talking about? You mean the fart? Ah, everyone does that."

I never knew that. So I started paying attention and discovered that he was absolutely right. Heavens, even I could make those sounds come out of me. It opened up a new level of acceptance and understanding of this thing that the average person apparently does at least 14 times a day (although a very close unnamed relative of mine swears that she does not).

As years passed, there were numerous incidents of inappropriate gaseous releases by other people around me, mostly men. I was always fascinated by how liberated they seemed to feel when they just outright *let one go*, as if wanting to share their good fortune with the rest of us. Typically, I'd just shake my head and mutter, "That's disgusting." I knew from the imaginary *Book of Proper*, which my mother often cited, that some things in life were reserved for private and there were others that ladies just didn't do. For the most part, I heeded those words.

One notable exception to my adherence to this set of principles occurred on an early morning when I was leaving the house to work at the golf course at 6:00 a.m. I jumped on my bike and realized something wasn't right. The popcorn kernels from the night before seemed to be still popping in my belly. To ease this discomfort I lifted my left cheek off the bike seat and with a bit of pressure let some of that bad air out. It didn't leave silently.

Satisfied, I sat back on my seat. To my horror, a head suddenly popped up from behind some trash cans. My neighbour politely greeted me with, "Good morning, Carole."

Mortified, I awkwardly regained my balance on the bike and vowed to show more respect in the future for the teachings of my mother.

In the spring of 1990 when I was pregnant with Alena, I declared that I'd had enough of the self-control thing. I was going to allow myself to enjoy two bacon double cheeseburgers at my weekly visit to the local fast food joint, spread peanut butter on my toast with bacon, and not fret nearly as much about exercising as when I was expecting the boys. I was determined to enjoy the benefits of being pregnant one last time, free from worry of the weight gain.

And did I ever. I remember commiserating with my friend Marcia one weekend, confiding in her that I had gained thirteen pounds. In a compassionate voice, she reassured me with, "Thirteen pounds? That's not bad for five months."

Reluctantly, I corrected her. Thirteen pounds was what I had gained since my last doctor's appointment.

Needless to say, I had a considerable amount of weight to lose after Alena was born. In my desperate effort to get some immediate results I decided to try out the latest promo for quick and easy weight loss. In secrecy, I went out and bought a carton of the canned chocolate flavoured milkshakes that promised to help you shrink fast. I figured I would drink them for breakfast and lunch and then cap off the day by enjoying Joe's home-cooked dinner. I hoped this would be what I needed to kick-start the weight loss. No weighing-in in front of a stranger, no stripping down in an open room and no public proclamations that went like, "Hello, my name is Carole Bertuzzi Luciani and I am a fat f**k."

So for a stretch of seven days I faithfully consumed those modified chocolate shakes, all the time visualizing the baby fat quickly shrinking. But there was one side effect that I had not anticipated. An inordinate amount of gaseous substance was accumulating in my belly. In the privacy of my room, I could be found rolling my clenched fists down my torso in hopes of releasing the toxins within. My goodness, it was painful ... both the ache and the odour. But I consoled myself by remembering Nona's advice: "You just gotta let it go."

One day about a week into the regime, I had to go to the mall. I was driving Joe's little puddle jumper, a Honda Prelude. Just as I was prowling for a parking spot, my insides started to grumble. I proceeded to *blow up a storm* and as I began to roll the window down to send the sulfuric fumes into the atmosphere, a familiar face came from out from nowhere and leaned through the open window into the car to kiss me.

OH MY GOODNESS. I WANT TO DIE ON THE SPOT AND DISAPPEAR INTO THE VINYL OF THE SEAT.

I slammed on the brakes. It was our friend Louie. A barrage of indignant thoughts bounced around in my brain. What business did he have being in Oakville, living, as he did, in Hamilton? He could have gotten run over jumping out like that! At the time any inane thought would have done to divert my feelings of mortification. Sitting there in my idling car, a pleasant conversation ensued as he rested his crossed arms comfortably on the window frame. To hide my intense embarrassment I vowed not to execute the primal scream until our goodbyes and I had found a spot to park.

It was 10 years later when I had the courage to ask if he remembered anything particular about that encounter at the mall. He assured me he didn't. I'm still not certain if he was just being polite and a gracious guy but whatever the truth was, I had to be thankful that either his long-term memory was short or his sense of smell was dull.

A Little Respect Please

*O*ur friends Pat and Dave hosted a party of family and friends.

As the evening progressed, more and more alcohol was consumed by the attendees and although I drank only water, I too, soon reached my saturation point. But mostly I just couldn't stay awake any longer. So we left the party before it peaked.

The next day we called to thank them for their hospitality and indulged in a sort of *postmortem* review of the evening.

"Carole, it's too bad you went home early because the party really picked up after you left. You missed the best part."

Upset that I missed the fun I responded, "Why? What happened?"

Dave went on to inform me of the highlight:

"Well of course my family got into the sauce and you never know where that's going to lead. My sister Reta and my daughter Nicky started getting into it and were yapping back and forth.

Finally my daughter had had enough of her aunt's comments. She stared down at my sister and said, "Reta, why don't you just F**k off."

Reta was so shocked by what she had heard, all she could do was glare back at Nicky and say, "Nicky where do you get off on calling me Reta ... I'm your aunt. I think I deserve some respect.""

A Revealing First Impression

My brother-in-law Richie makes me laugh. Not only is he an extremely funny guy (even though he repeats his good lines ad nauseam) but he is almost always doing something to get a laugh. Regrettably such acts are often at my expense. It rarely matters as I inevitably end up laughing.

Early on in his marriage to my sister, I was invited over to their place to meet some friends of theirs who were visiting from Montreal. Claire and Clive were a couple I had heard a lot about and I looked forward to finally meeting them in person.

Since it was summer, I was decked out into the typical fashion of the late 1970's: ultra high gym shorts and a tight tank top. Looking back I see that I revealed a whole whack of skin in those days.

As soon as I entered the backyard where everyone was lounging, Richie started to introduce me to his friends. Being my natural congenial self, I smiled and eagerly approached them to shake their hand and begin the friendly banter and conversation.

Unbeknownst to me as I stepped toward them, Richie had quietly snuck in behind me. Just as I reached out to extend my hand, I suddenly felt something tug at the elastic waistband of my shorts. Before I could reach back to determine the cause I felt a surprisingly odd sensation.

Instantly I realized the culprit … Richie had dropped a toad down the back of my pants. With no time to filter or figure out the protocol, I yanked both my shorts and underwear off in record speed.

Within seconds of my introductions there I was squirming, yelping and dancing before their friends … and butt naked from the waist down. Mortified, I immediately ran for cover. As I tore off (good choice of words) all I could hear from Clive was, "Oh Carole, come back. I was just getting to know you. And I really like you so far."

To this day, Richie still ranks that one at the top of the list.

P.S. Just last Sunday I shared this story with my sister and brother-in-law. In doing so, we recounted other memories of Claire and Clive. It was decided that we should try to contact them to reconnect. I immediately started a *Google* search to find an address for them. Unfortunately there were three listed, so it wasn't immediately possible.

Three days later, Sharon received a call from Claire. She wanted to let them know that Clive had passed away. He had died on Monday … just one day after our reminiscing.

Gardening Tips to Raise a Child

As a landscaper I've discovered how the planning, preparation and maintenance of a garden is a lot like parenting.

Here are some of the valuable tips I've dug up:

* To grow a beautiful healthy garden requires a major investment of your time and energy

* Have a plan for your garden with parameters you need to work within

* Never plant a garden to emulate your neighbours

* Determine the best environment for optimal growth of your plants and remember plants bloom at different times

* Just because a plant isn't doing well one season, doesn't mean you have to pull it out

* Although plants need their space to flourish they still require ongoing nourishment and attention

* Even if you prefer a garden that grows wild, at some point pruning is necessary

*Just because there are weeds all around … doesn't mean there isn't a bud lost somewhere in the middle looking for light

* Be patient, plants need time to achieve their full growth and beauty

* Be open to sharing gardening resources with others … you will discover while your garden is unique, the problem it might present, is not

* The greatest joy is sitting back and savouring the beauty of your garden.

P.S. Remember, *garden work*, like parenting, is never ending.

For the Love of the Game

As a parent of three, each passionate about athletics, I have earned every spread inch of my 'bleacher butt' over the past 20 years. It is a result of watching hundreds of games at various age levels and tiers of competition in a multitude of sports … except hockey. I told my kids they didn't have organized hockey in our town.

Joe and I could have retired to an island by now had we not financed the registration fees, equipment, lessons, training, travel expenses and sport-specific fundraisers over the years, not to mention the expenses incurred from every weekend tournament. It didn't help my financial situation that I also went to games involving relatives or kids of friends. Heck, I go to games even if I just know the kid because he works at the mall … I really do need a life. But I enjoy supporting young people doing what they love, especially my own.

Part of the experience of being *one of the parents* on any team is just that, being *one of the parents*. As our children gel on the field, court, diamond or ice, we form our own team with bonds just as deep. Our positions in the stands are clear. We are there to support our child and her team. And will do anything towards that goal.

Like our children, we too, play different roles drawing on our individual skill sets. We coordinate the tailgate, supply the half-time cookies in the stands, take the photos, distribute the clappers, book the team meal or dish out the post game comfort to the athletes and to each other.

Pre-game is different for all of us. Some nervously pace while others have their rituals not to be disturbed. Personally, I remain relatively calm as I am confident I will never be called out of the bleachers to play. After the game we are as worn out and exhausted as the players. And of course there's the post-mortem, the ad nauseam discussions full of woulda-coulda-shouldas. Trust me, it doesn't matter how many times and ways you hash it out, they will NEVER WIN THAT GAME they lost. Or with happier finishes we congratulate each other with such enthusiasm it's like we played the game ourselves.

While some parents busy themselves with stats, strategizing or screaming at the officials, I work hardest at coordinating my outfit of team colours with matching noisemaking accessories. And I usually cheer openly and positively ... at least since the one game when the ref approached me to issue a warning after I loudly questioned his call. Such spirited passion is necessary because if the team's important to a child, it's important to a parent.

We attend the games out of desire but also out of duty because it is written in the parent handbook under *additional responsibilities*. The manual had obviously been rewritten for us baby boomers because my parents never came to my games ... and interestingly I haven't ended up in therapy. I often wonder if maybe we were better off because of it.

Our family has been fortunate to enjoy the highs of a few great championships. They were exciting, satisfying and mem-orable experiences that we will treasure forever. And I'm certain with each telling of the tale the game conditions will be magnified thus elevating the magnitude of the win.

But not all seasons have been successful; some of them weren't even fun; and a select few were downright painful to endure for a variety of reasons. Issues typically revolve around coaching decisions and their impact on our child ... as it should. We are their investors, their advocates and personal cheerleaders. That's where our interest lies. Although we can't fix the problem for them, it is our parental yen to feel *for* them, the essence of empathic harmony.

Most parents live by the credo: *when my baby's not happy, I'm not happy.* There will always be broken hearts, shattered dreams and emotional debris for us to clean up. And that is when it is most challenging (but also when most important life lessons are learned). Our child's disappointment hurts us significantly more than our own. It's an emotional roller coaster ride requiring mandatory helmets and chest protection. Regardless how painful it is we keep going back because they are our babies to love and protect. It is our *raison d'être*. Although we may not always have answers for them, we do have open arms.

But today I got a *nudge* backed by a whisper, "Psst. Hey, you. Pay attention to this."

Having coffee at Tim Horton's we sat beside an older couple (just slightly older than us). The man initiated the conversation with us after he noticed Joe's team-wear.

"I see you're from Laurier. You here for the basketball (Canadian University National Basketball Championship)?

"Yes, we are. How about you? Are you following any of it?"

"Oh yeah we haven't missed a game and will go to all the rest. We're actually Mac fans."

"Mac? Really? And they're not even in it. Do you have a daughter who plays?"

"Nope."

"Were you once players?"

"No, neither of us is the least bit athletic. But we never miss the Nationals. And for sure we'll be in Calgary next year."

"Really? Even if your team's not in it?"

"Oh yeah we go to every game of the season … men's and women's. We even write the blog for the team."

"Wow. Good for you. I guess I have to ask … Why?"

"Because we just love the game."

As I left Tim's I was still thinking about that conversation with Neil and Eleanor … so much so I left my purse behind (thankfully I did retrieve it).

It made me realize that sometimes we get so caught up in fulfilling parental responsibilities and *being there* for them, that along the way we have neglected an essential element in the mix … to just sit back and enjoy the game. As a society we put so much focus on success, with winning being the direct route. And winning is both the reward for performance and the prelude to happiness. It's difficult to move beyond that.

So today I pledge that I will happily continue to support my children as they pursue their passion for playing. But once they're done, I'm going to adopt Eleanor and Neil's philosophy to show support for the sheer love of the game. The *Founders of Sport* would really like that.

But for now, my arms will remain open to embrace the elation of their highs and absorb the tears of their lows. After all, I'm getting really good at it. I guess that's because I have the longest arms on the team and lots of practise.

P.S. Just in case you're thinking I'm a coddling, doting and over protective mom … only as required.

Old School Safety

*W*hen my first maternity leave was over, I returned to work on a part-time basis. The childcare arrangements were split between a woman in the neighborhood and my parents.

One day I drove to my parents' home to pick-up Dante and although I knew my mom was working I was surprised to notice that my dad's car was also gone.

I was puzzled because I had the car seat. Where could he possibly have gone with a six month old and no car seat? It was the time before cell phones and I had no access into their house, so I nervously jumped in the car and headed home.

I fretted the whole way creating worrisome scenarios involving my dad and Dante. I was stumped. I prayed that once I got home, there might at least be a message on the answering machine with an explanation.

As I pulled onto our street I was both aghast and relieved to see my dad's car parked in front. Having no clue what that meant in relation to my baby, I parked the car and ran into the house.

Upon entering the kitchen there sat my dad reading the paper with Dante on his lap. It took a few seconds for the scene to register but then I erupted. "What are you doing here? No. Wait, how did you get here?"

Without a qualm he answered, "I drove. How the hell did you think I got here?"

"No. I mean how did you get Dante here, without the car seat?"

"The same way I got all you kids around. I laid him on the

floor in the back next to the hump."

"AGGGGGGGHHHHHHHHHHHHHHH ... my BA-BY!!!!!!"

I couldn't believe what I had just heard. My precious first born flopped on the floor of his Noni's car. "Did he cry? Did he scream? Did he lie still in fear? Was he uncomfortable? What if ... what if ... what if ...?" and I rhymed off a string of all that could've happened.

Then one glance at the two of them made me realize they were perfectly content and feeling no ill effects of the drive. Dante, who was sitting comfortably in the arms of my dad was sucking on his bottle of formula as my dad sucked on his own bottle ... of IPA beer.

They both gave me the look that said, "Relax. What's all the fuss about? We're here aren't we?"

Cleanliness ... Next to Godliness

As I sat through a very long-winded Mass today, I was entertained by two beautiful little girls.

At one point, the two-and-a-half year old grabbed a wet *wipe* from behind her mom's back. She proceeded to very diligently clean her entire section of the pew, wiped the bottom of her mom's denim bag and then the baby seat. Almost done, she then scooped her baby sister's bottle and gave it a good clean. Her last effort to make sure everything within reach was cleansed, she twisted the dirty bit of wet *wipe* around the nipple and stuffed it in her sister's mouth.

Both little girls were overjoyed ... the parents were oblivious.

Italian Logic

When my husband and I were newly married we would make occasional overnight visits to my Nona's apartment. Since there was only one bedroom, she provided us with bedding for the living room hardwood floor.

To assure us it would be much more comfortable than we were anticipating, she offered: "Ah *figlia* (loved one in Italian), it's not really lika sleeping on the ground. We're three floors upa."

I Think I Can Dance

I'm probably the best private dancer I know. Wait, not the kind you're thinking of. I mean dancing alone in my own company. You see, I have a lot of Tina Turner in me. OK maybe I'm being facetious but with music blaring and all obstacles out of the way, I can really *do my thing*. If nothing else, I'm good enough to be one of her backup dancers.

My earliest memories of dance (other than the painful ballet and tap debacles) are visions of my mother doing the Charleston in the crowded kitchen of our small home to *In the Mood* blaring from the radio. And look out if my dad was around because she relished having a partner. I was often her default. She was particularly good at the *bent-over-swinging-knee-action*, whatever that was called.

I learned the *Mash Potatoes* at the Marrone house; the *Twist* from my older cousin Marilyn; and the *Tarantella* from watching older relatives at weddings. But the practising of all the steps only took place in the privacy of my own room with my pink plastic, flip-up 45 RPM record player blasting.

As I got older I wore down the basement carpet perfecting dances with names like *Shingaling, Boogaloo,* the *Jerk, Watusi* and every other orchestrated routine that was *all the go*, at the time. I spent hours studying shows like *Shindig* and *Hullabaloo* to learn each sequence of steps. I was particularly good at the *Freddy* with my long arms and the *Shuffle* with my long legs. If a partner was needed there was always my sister, a friend, aunt or cousin more than willing shake it up with me. And as the tallest among them, I was the one who led (a designation Joe still struggles with).

All that practising really didn't matter because I knew chances were slim I'd ever be called upon to display my prowess. Sock hops at our all girls school demanded a partner … of the opposite sex. It was torture to stand on the sidelines twitchin' to the tunes, having to wait to be asked. It didn't help that most boys were shorter than me. And unfortunately it most often didn't happen until the last song of the night … *Stairway to Heaven, Let it Be* or *Hey Jude.* And besides it didn't matter what kind of a *groove* you were in, that's when the nuns came to life with their bells and their warnings to, "Make room for the Holy Ghost."

I still do my best moves when on my own with the music dialled loud enough to feel the pounding in my chest. And once I get the beat, I quickly sync it with my finger snaps … loud enough to awaken my snoring husband.

But beyond that, at least I'm now confident enough to jump up at any opportunity to dance whether I have a partner or not. Truthfully, the way I cover the floor, I'm better off on my own, even though it is way more fun when my dancing queen friends join me.

If one of my friends shouts out any dance name, within seconds we're on our feet showing off our version of the moves. We don't even need the music. Unlike my kids, who claim to dance all night with moves that have no names. When I ask about what the steps are called, the typical answer is, "I dunno. It's just dancing." So boring.

Although I hold a deep rooted belief that I am a great dancer, my kids would argue otherwise (at least judging by how they mock me). They mostly imitate my shoulder lift moves (easily done from even a seated position while driving) and how I drop my mouth open. And apparently I am *so forty years ago* when I dance.

I won't let their criticism deter me. But now that I think about it and my self-professed similarity to Tina, perhaps I do have some work to do ... a bit more leg work in the gym and I'm certain we'll be cloned.

Blood Work: A Test for Patients

*I'*m always amazed when I arrive at the blood lab at 7:03 a.m. (it opens at 7 a.m.) and discover I'm #35 ... surely they must camp out overnight in the hallway.

Looking around at the sea of glum faces, I think I've seen more joyful expressions in a funeral home. As I sit studying the room with my pre-breakfast smirk, I slowly get to know them ...

*the *fasters* ... having fasted for at least 12 hours, they are just downright cranky with no concern about exposing just how miserable they really look or feel. Perhaps I too am guilty of this as I sit here dreaming about my hit of caffeine.

*the *employed* ... a quick blood test on the way to work but seeing the overflow of impatient people pouring into the hallway, they know they'll be late and they're annoyed, so out come the Blackberries and laptops.

*the *sleepers* ... some have not quite woken up yet as they lounge stretched out on the vinyl chairs napping. They really don't care how long it takes; just be sure to wake them when their number's called.

*the *competitive* ... who, although they arrived in the parking lot seconds after you, dashed ahead to the door, a quick foot race down the stairs in time to grab the preceding number ... only to wait. And as they do, their eyes dart around the room, their feet tapping and body squirming. I love it when I ultimately walk out past them, pressing my Band-Aid to my arm as they sit waiting for the technician in the next cubicle.

*the *sighers* ... who having risen to fill in their form, discover upon returning to their seat, that it has been occupied by another waiting patient.

*the *frightened* … who suffer from either the language barrier, concern for their health or the dreaded balonephobia - the fear of needles. You actually think I made that up don't you?

*the *support group* … who really have no place taking up space on either the scarce selection of seating or in the room at all. They're there to offer moral support to their friend, spouse or parent and are typically the most jovial because they've eaten and they know they will not have to roll up a sleeve or drop their pants as directed. But I do like it when I realize they are not holding a number.

*and finally, the *experienced* … who have been through this many times. They know the drill. They come armed with their crafts, sudoku or favourite book. They're in no hurry as they've blocked the morning off for the outing. And if anyone is going to engage in friendly conversation, my bets are on them.

OK, I gotta go. I just heard the receptionist stutter the bastardized version of Bertuzzi Luciani. I'm up.

Next stop is getting my coffee … just a half a cup though. No heavy lifting.

Are You Paying Attention?

$\mathcal{W}$hen I was younger I was frequently on the receiving end of my father's pointed elbow jabbing into my side along with the booming words: "If you'd just stop and pay attention, you just might learn something."

Of course I dismissed it as I did most things uttered by my parents.

But looking back, they remain a personal favourite as a guideline for life.

Although his sentiments were directed to me as the learner, they are equally as important words for the teacher (or parent).

It wasn't until I was in the tenth grade that someone noticed that there was something different about me amid the sea of dark uniforms, seated in straight rows at our strict, academically inclined all girls school.

One day in Geography class, Sister Elizabeth Ann issued instructions for the term project. She outlined the requirements of both research and essay, stressing the importance of a well written paper.

Before the end of class, she beckoned me to her desk and said, "Carole I want you to complete this project in whatever way you believe you can best convey your ideas. I encourage you to use your imagination."

Of course it caught me by surprise. Why had she chosen me as an exemption to the rule? Although I was somewhat confused, my mind was already swirling with ideas and I was excited about the possibilities for the project. Never before had a teacher recognized that perhaps I didn't grasp information like my *A*-achieving friends; possibly all that doodling represented a more visual inclination; and maybe all those times I acted out, I had already tuned out from both boredom and too much information that was merely noise rattling in my head.

Label it as you wish, but that brief conversation in 1969 punctured the smallest opening into my mind. Although it would still take years to completely understand and embrace my personal learning style and unleash my creativity, it was my teacher who paid enough attention to me to recognize it.

I remain eternally grateful to her.

"Can You Come Out to Play?"

_N_othing draws me out of a rut like the early hints of spring. It must go back to being born in April and left outside in my carriage (apparently that is what they did in the 1950's) to enjoy the crisp air and brief glimpses of sunshine. Since then, spring has remained my favourite time of the year.

Oh to wake up on a Saturday, as a child, look outside and see but scant blobs of leftover snow. It didn't matter what the temperature was … the pavement was calling.

A quick scoot outside to get the bike out of the cold dark garage where it had stayed leaning up against the wall for the past five months. Its retrieval meant getting a rag to dust the cobwebs, awakening the tires from their deflated state of rest and then the ultimate: flipping the bike onto its seat and dripping oil into the chain as I wound it into a frenzy. The only other tweaking to be done before hitting the streets was mounting the cold vinyl seat to determine just how many inches I had grown over the winter. When I outgrew the full extension of the chrome seat pole, it was time to plead my case for a bigger bike.

There were no phone calls to friends to beckon them out of the house. If they weren't already out or at least looking out the window, all you had to do was ride up the driveway and yell, "Hey, Marilyn can you come out to play?" And guess what? She didn't even have to ask permission. She'd grab her jacket and the next stop would be her garage to refresh her bike from hibernation. This would continue until every kid on the street was riding their wheels to escape the confines of Whyte Avenue and explore the rest of our town, Thorold.

Part of that first ride included a visit to Al's Cycle Shop on Front Street to check out the latest acquisitions in bicycle accessories. It was never just the goods that kept us wishing and roaming his hardwood floors, but the smell of rubber tires inhaled with every breath. After being measured up for the next size CCM (not to buy, just to record in case the day came) we'd head back onto the streets making sure our tires met every puddle discarded by winter as our legs hung freely in the air to avoid the splash.

From there it would be back to our driveways where we'd drop our bikes to the ground with wheels left spinning an head off to search for our *play things* not seen or used since the fall.

Minutes later, we'd gather once again to survey the goods and consider our options … requiring great deliberation by all involved.

Hmm, how could we spend our day?

Would we skip first? Linda got a new rope for her last birthday and it hasn't been unravelled yet. It'll be stiff but a few pepper turns and it will loosen up. Two already volunteered to be the ever-enders because they didn't want to scuff their new Keds. And a couple were already recounting and reciting last years songs like: *Apples, peaches, pears and plums … tell me when your birthday comes.*

Was the playground dry enough for 7-Up baseball? We had enough gloves for at least the fielders … we could easily share. Our old wooden bat's broken but it will do. We'll just have to shorten our grip. And we can use that ball the janitor threw off the school roof. We could start out with our small group but others will for sure join us in a matter of time. And wouldn't it be fun to play around all the mud.

Was the ground soft enough to cut a hole on the boulevard for Allies? It seemed most still had their Crown Royal bag of marbles from last year and we could pair up into teams. We'd have to go easy on our finger fronts though because they're still tender from a coddled and mittened winter.

Or, wait, maybe we could just go across to the school and play *one ball* against the wall ... we'd bring the other two red, white and blue striped balls along for once we got our skills back. We all still knew the words and the actions. That would be fun, as long as the boys didn't come around to spoil the fun heaving their *Indian rubber balls*. And just in case we break all the world records in *two-ball* counting by fives, there was always the ball in the stocking whipped around to the verse: *Hello hello hello sir.*

How about we decorate our bikes? Maybe just start with gripping the clothes pegs and old baseball cards from last season onto the spokes. And there's no problem if your bike has a flat. We can ride double. The extra weight will make the cards flap even louder.

At the very least we could hit the playground to reacquaint ourselves with the frozen metal of the swings and slides.

Oh yeah, we'd huddle together staring at the complete assortment of neighbourhood *goods*. Collectively we surveyed the condition of each item and shared our ideas for the day ahead. We never fought or argued about it because we knew by day's end each one would eventually be used. Tiring from one activity we'd quickly move onto the next gathering both other kids and momentum along the way.

And as we continued to make the most of our day playing, unbeknownst to us we were negotiating, gathering resources, cooperating and problem solving. We organized logistics, pooled our knowledge, made decisions, worked together, competed and experienced the ultimate in team-building skills. And we had fun doing it. There was no trophy, ribbon or recognition at stake, other than perhaps bragging rights until the next day's events.

In between our rounds of fun, we'd dash home to pee (or not) and if time permitted, grab something to eat on the run like those great *mangicake* sandwiches on white bread that our one non-Italian friend's mom provided. Eventually we would return home. Our moms knew we would and they also knew just by the smell of the outdoors we dragged in that spring had arrived.

Our cheeks would be burned by the fresh spring breeze; cold to touch yet somehow heated by the sweat of our brow from all the running around; noses dripped into the frozen crust that had settled at our nostrils; and our faces beamed expressions of sheer exhilaration from a wonderful day spent outside, with friends, doing what we loved the most ... playing to exhaustion.

Whether or not we still had our jacket, baseball glove or bike with us, was another story. It didn't matter. It would all be found the next day exactly where we left it.

Ah, I still love spring and what it brings. I welcome another one back into my life so I can look forward to more days enjoyed outside.

And I might even get my bike out. Guaranteed I didn't get taller over this past winter. But sadly I bet I won't be meeting up with many young kids out on the pavement ... they'll be in all those cars whizzing by en route to another scheduled *play* activity.

Doing Anything September 11th?

A year ago I met up with an old friend who had lost her husband in the 9-11 tragedy. To recap our brief conversation, she mentioned how her dream was to get everyone to acknowledge the *day* by doing a random act of kindness. She envisioned it as a global way to honour the victims by doing one small thing to better our world. I loved the idea. And I didn't wait for a proclamation to act upon it.

After sharing the idea with my friend Carol Ann we decided to do something we refer to as *giving a garden casserole* (yes, you're right. I have already mentioned it).

We then visited Holy Sepulchre Cemetery in Hamilton armed with our tools and energized to beautify as many forgotten graves as we could. By the end of our stay we had tended to over 30 such overgrown and neglected areas. And there wasn't one complaint.

The beauty was not just in the results of our labour but also that we were able to toil undisturbed and execute our random act with little organizational effort. It was so pleasurable and rewarding we have decided to return next year with our own Yard Duty crew.

So, how will you make a positive contribution to the day? It doesn't have to be anything grandiose or time consuming … just use your imagination and do it. No handshakes, no headlines, no hoopla. Trust me, you'll feel good.

Can You Give Me Directions?

I'm not a fan of the GPS. The pet name we have for our dashboard diva is Myda … as mighta get there, mighta not.

Although I do whatever I can to avoid her, my husband loves her. He trusts that with her help there will never be a situation resulting in, "You can't there from here." And besides, it gets him off the hook from stopping to ask for directions.

Unfortunately there are times when I must rely on her directionally-enhanced knowledge. But I do so reluctantly because I find her to be bland and boring company. And like any person you find annoying, I easily tire of her and her emotionless drone. Therefore I'm quick to tune her out and ignore her orders. However it does not go unnoticed.

"One keel-om-metre, turn right.

Turn right.

Tuuurn right.

Turn right now.

NOW."

Oops, I missed the turn. My music's too loud.

"Re-cal-cu-lating. Now travel six kee-lom-metres and turn left."

At that point I poke at her until she's off, never to hear the words, "A-rriving at dest-tin-ation."

Personally I relate better to visual cues or at least more user-friendly directions that might go like this:

"Get on the road that cuts through town but make sure the

lake is to your left, because remember that means south.

You'll pass the new mall. Oh, it's Scratch and Save today.

Check your speedometer because there's always a cop hiding just past the bridge. Just smile and wave.

Keep going for about the length of one song then you'll see one of those blue tourist signs. I forget what it says, but I think it's got a golfer on it, or at least some sort of an image. Pull off there.

Now go towards the big glass building on your right. I know they're looking for summer staff if your son's interested. Apparently the pay's pretty good.

As you pass it, look at the beautiful lights on their trees. I love them. They have great landscaping too. I wish I could cut an edge like that around my garden. I think they use a machine.

Now go just past the school. Oh that's where that Olympic runner went in the 1980's. It's public. There's no crucifix.

You'll see a row of light coloured stuccoed townhouses … you know not really pink but not quite tan with a peach hue. I think it's a new shade out this year.

There's one unit with the blossom tree … well actually there are two but you'll know which one needs pruning. Slow down when you see that one. I should really leave a business card for Yard Duty.

Look to the unit two or three to the right of it with the funky mailbox. That's where *that* woman lives we've spoken about … you know. OK, I'll tell you when you get here.

Now look across the street from it. Ours is the one with the garage door opened but no car … there's just no room for it. Check out some of the junk though. You might be interested.

See you when you get here. The wine's cooling."

It just makes the trip so much more interesting.

Now if the GPS could develop a bit of a personality maybe I'd want to spend more time with her.

Squeeze Play at First Base

*J*ust two weeks after I gave birth to Vince, I was raring to get back to playing baseball. I felt good, had no pains and didn't have a ton of excess weight … OK so maybe I had just grown used to it. Besides with two children under two I was desperate to get out of the house.

The only concern I had in getting back was what to do with the jiggling of the stretched skin that gently flapped with any movement. It was like wearing a loose sash that continually needed to be repositioned.

Pondering my problem I thought of a possible solution to help me with the ease and comfort of returning to the game.

I asked my mom if she might have a type of panty girdle I could borrow. Please understand my mother has a supporting cast from her past that could fill three drawers. One of her favourite sayings is: "You can never have too many corsets."

She said she did have an old one I could try so I went over and picked it up. Later at home I looked more closely at it and shuddered at the thought of using it as shrink wrap.

The night of the scheduled return, my baseball friend Lorna dropped by.

I told her my plan and we decided it couldn't do any harm to give it a try.

But getting into it was a challenge. Think of the effort required to squeeze 20 pounds of flesh into a 10 pound casing. It was extremely difficult, the most strenuous activity I had had in months but, "Ahhh, I did it." With sweat pouring off my face I got into my uniform and we headed to the game.

By the time we arrived at the diamond, I had a stomach ache. I prayed I wouldn't have to bend over for any grounders at first. It hurt that much. It was the same feeling I had when I tried my first somersault as an overweight eight year old. My belly hurt so much I NEVER attempted one again. Honest.

When it was my turn at bat, I managed to swing easily as there was nothing to impede my range ... but c'mon, that fat had to go somewhere. After a few pitches I did hit the ball but interestingly it took me a few seconds to start my motion to first base. Once I managed to actually take off, I kept looking behind me for the loaded wagon that surely was hitched to my upper thighs ... obviously the landing pad for the fat.

I did eventually make it to first. That's only because I had not lost my hitting title, in my break from the game, for hitting the *longest single* in the league. This just meant I could hit it out of the park but only run fast enough to get to first base.

I never wore the panty girdle again but it did serve as the incentive I needed to start shedding that *baby fat*.

Unfortunately, that was 25 years ago ... and I'm still trying.

The Logical Listing ...

$\mathcal{O}$ne morning, while still in bed, I was preparing the day's checklist for Joe and the kids. I was going out and wanted to make sure everything was accounted for and they all knew what had to be done.

I nudged Joe to review the list with him.

I then remembered one more thing ...

"Oh, and Vince has to cut Dorothy's lawn. But if it rains or he can't do it this afternoon, have him call her."

Half sleeping, Joe asked, "Do you have her number?"

Yeah, it's in my book ... under *N*."

Now fully awake he questioned me. "Under *N*? Their name is Grant. Why would I ever think to look there?"

I answered in a no nonsense, matter of fact tone: "*N* for neighbour."

Laughing, he threw back "That's the most ridiculous thing I've heard. What would ever make you think that's logical?"

Unwaveringly, I explained that it made perfect sense to me.

"I easily could forget her name, but I would never forget she was a neighbour." Point made.

But he wasn't buying it. It had really struck a chord with him and he continued laughing about what he labelled my illogical thinking.

"That makes no sense. Yet another example of your skewed thinking. That's right up there with keeping your sweaters in the freezer and always buying a medium black coffee, knowing you only ever drink half."

That evening we were with my sister and her husband. Of course the joke of the phone listing was shared. Richard wholeheartedly agreed with Joe. They both thought it was absolutely ridiculous.

Sharon, however, did not share in their reaction. When they finally stopped dissecting the hilarity of the incident, she calmly said, "I don't see what's so funny about that. It is exactly the way I do it. It makes perfect sense to me."

I thanked her and was comforted by the allegiance.

But, then I wondered ... is it familial logic or female logic?

What do you think?

Proceed With Caution

While in university, I joined a group of friends on one of those rites of passage for students in Ontario, a bus trip to the Quebec Winter Carnival in February. It was freezing, of course, but we were pumped for this exciting experience and ready for a good time. We signed up without giving a thought about what to expect. High school trips had always been well organized, and while accommodations weren't necessarily lavish, they had always been clean and spacious. We trusted that the same standards would apply for this trip.

After a long and noisy bus ride, and having sung one too many rounds of *One Hundred Bottles of Beer on the Bus*, we were surprised when it pulled into a subdivision and squeezed into the driveway of a cozy little bungalow. With stunned looks on our faces, all 50 of us grabbed our packs and got off the bus to check out what was apparently going to serve as our accommodation. I wondered if it was going to be like the animated cartoon where the character steps into a tiny tent in the desert, only to find a giant palace inside, complete with servants and a harem.

Unfortunately, that was not to be the case. Rather, what we soon discovered was that to make some extra cash, an entrepreneurial family had made a few minor changes to their home and opened it to busloads of partying students. To maximize the number of bodies they could house, they had created five partitioned rooms in the basement, each of which was jammed with five sets of bunks. Fifty students in a one basement with one washroom. Unbelievable! With barely room to stand, (and no space to change your mind let alone your clothes) it was very clear that we would not be spending much time there.

So we hit the streets and joined the rest of partying Quebec City. We strolled through the slush; we sipped wine from our wine skins; we excitedly talked to strangers, and we checked out every pub in the city core. With plans to avoid our crowded digs at all costs, (I guess that's what the owners had banked on) we managed to take in every activity planned for this festive event.

Heading toward the waterfront, we noticed that a sizable crowd had gathered and decided to check it out. As we got closer, we realized that they were there to watch the great ice boat race. Most of the crowd was standing well back from the embankment at the water's edge. Just in front of them appeared to be part of a construction site. This was a dangerous location, as evidenced by the many not-so-subtle signs around that read: *DANGER! DEFENSE D'ENTRER* (loosely translated - stay the heck away). Yet despite these warnings, there was a group of individuals that had somehow managed to work its way right up to the water's edge.

Initially opting for safety, we stood with the first group. Within minutes, however, we all decided we wanted a better view and decided to join the front row of spectators at the edge. This meant we had to cross over the construction area, a span of about 15 feet. So one by one, we stepped along the six-inch wide planks, which were spaced evenly across the site. Between each of the parallel boards were large green sheets of plastic. It certainly looked easy enough; well over 100 people had already made it across ahead of us, so we figured it couldn't be that hard.

Babbi went first; she was followed by Marcia, Debbie, Peggy and then Joanne. This left me to bring up the rear. Never having been particularly graceful, I carefully watched each of them as they crossed, making note of the best methods for negotiating the narrow plank. When it came to my turn, I took a deep breath and warily made my first step. My mukluks were heavy with moisture. My left foot carefully followed. With eight feet still to go, I was bringing the right one around again when my foot slipped off the plank. Before I knew it, I was straddling it like I was on the seat of a teeter totter ... only it hurt a heck of a lot more.

Prior to this moment, I hadn't given any thought to what might be hidden beneath the green sheets of plastic. I learned in an instant ... it was air! Catching my breath for the second time in a few short minutes, I gingerly looked down through the hole in the plastic.

What I saw was a deep zone of darkness that had swallowed up my legs. Having no choice but to give myself a couple of seconds to allow my eyes to adjust, I realized that beneath me was the rocky bottom of the construction site 20 feet below. As I sat frozen in fear I couldn't hear my heart pound because of the roar of laughter around me. The hoots of my intoxicated friends were punctuated by comments like, "How could you be so klutzy?" "We made it okay, what happened to you?"

Hearing all this, the crowd turned their backs on the boat races in order to tune into the exciting drama that was unfolding right in front of them. They joined in the laughter as they caught the improbable sight of me marooned on the skinny board. It was easy for them to laugh; they were not the ones getting slivers through damp and freezing jeans. Nor did they have to figure out how to get themselves back up on their feet and over to the other side. Had I been in their shoes, my reaction would likely have been the same, but it was my butt on the line (so to speak), and all I knew was that I didn't know what to do.

As I sat there with fear in my heart and terror in my eyes, I felt the wood crackle beneath me and I knew it didn't matter how funny it appeared ... I was in danger. I was aware that the rocks below me would mean a treacherous landing, and this realization just served to heighten my paralysis. Finally, someone clued in to my desperate state and passed me the end of a long branch. Instructions started flying from all directions. Tuning everyone out, I managed to gently lift my legs up through the ripped plastic and position myself sideways on the cracked plank. Holding the branch for reassurance, I slowly inched my way to the other side. To the cheers and clapping of the crowd of strangers, I breathed a great sigh of relief when my feet finally landed on firm ground. My friends (what friends?) were still laughing hysterically (all the alcohol had clearly fogged up their perceptions), and were of no use to me at all.

With the tightrope show over, everyone turned their attention back to the water and caught the tail end of the race. Although I looked like I, too, was watching, my mind was clamped on the realization that I still had to renegotiate the trip back over the plank. Fortunately, I made it safely and without incident, and we all ventured back into the city core. With everyone still enjoying the lingering effects of the evening, I trailed a few steps behind, comforting an ego that had taken a beating from the public embarrassment, and recovering from my brush with danger.

As my friends continued to revel in the delight of it, someone offhandedly summed up the experience ... "Carole, if it was safe ... the sign would have read: *SAFE!*"

Knowing they would never quite understand the trauma I had experienced, I slunk back to my skinny bunk in the sardine can, swearing that for the duration of our trip I would not set foot (or butt) on anything narrower than a toboggan.

Dear Ms. Media Personality

*Y*ou and I go waaaay back. I was in your TV viewing audience for your first show in the 1980's. There I sat on the bed with my newborn and I saw hope. Hope that I could survive the next three months of my maternity leave with something to look forward to watching each day and hope for me. I saw a lot of myself in you with your self deprecating style, your naturalness in relating to others and the fact that like myself, you were not a '10' based on society's skewed beauty scale. All of this gave me the nod to be my natural self in my own career.

I followed you closely over the years (real life did get in the way some seasons) and continued to cheer you on in all of your endeavours. I may not have always agreed with your responses, didn't necessarily approve of your celebrity gushing and may have winced at your opulent celebrations, but you did keep my interest. OK, now that I'm being honest with you, I'm really NOT a fan of your big giveaways. C'mon it's like looking through the window at a great party you weren't invited to. And your most favourite items ... maybe if I had your money I could develop a love affair with those things too. How about a segment on your 'favourite things from the dollar store'?

One year I even managed to score some seats for your show. It took days of patiently hovering over the phone pressing redial until a connection was made. Finally speaking with a real person my mood quickly meandered from sheer elation to panic when I discovered your required age for admission was 19. Our group of four included my sister, Mom, me and my niece who was only 18. My apologies, but I was not going to let this minute snag get in the way. I accepted the challenge and produced a fake ID for her. We were scanned, frisked and photographed but my simple homemade student card passed the test. I doubt I'd get away with it today.

Your show that day was about a dad who was 'coming out' to his family. Our mom, 74 at the time (now 91) quietly grimaced at the sensitive subject, but at least it prepared us for the other show we attended the next day, when together we had to endure 'secret sexual fantasies'!!

You strolled out in a beautiful shrimp coloured knit suit, twirled around and announced to great adoration and applause, "Size 8."

My mom, a seamstress, muttered, "Well, if that suit's an 8, I wanna shop where she shops." Don't worry, we managed to "Shhh" the fashion critic within her as we eagerly continued to cheer your every move. Truthfully, you could emerge wearing a potato sack and your fans would still roar wildly with great enthusiasm and admiration.

At the end of the show we lined up to get up close and personal with you the 'Beloved'. Although photos weren't allowed I asked you to you if it was OK to give you a hug? You responded, "Sure, mano-a-mano." To this day that remains one of my favourite claims to fame.

So, although we never did become the friends I secretly knew we could be nor did you ever did call to invite me to be your Canadian correspondent, I really wanted to send you a gift of my book: *"I have a story for you ..."* You would appreciate the honestly, humility and humour, all traits that I know you value. But sadly I have just discovered you are no longer accepting unsolicited packages in the mail, so all I can say is "You would have loved the gift I was going to send you." (Don't you hate that?)

Humbly, I realize you will never read this ... but heh I feel good writing it anyway.

Congratulations ... you continue to use your gifts to improve our world. And, I sincerely thank you for being a part of mine.

Carole Bertuzzi Luciani

The Wave of Destruction

One day, as part of my role at Camp Tawingo, I was asked to take the truck in for repairs. Ah, I looked forward to bouncing down Ravenscliffe Road in the vintage vehicle with tunes blaring.

When I arrived at the car dealership in Huntsville, I checked in and quickly found a spot to wait on the one available vinyl chair. I was perfectly content because I knew I had some interesting people-watching to enjoy over the course of my wait.

As my eyes wandered about the room, the guy next to me proceeded to chat me up. He figured he knew me so he might as well be friendly. He was obviously a local (as he seemed to know almost everyone), older than myself and was quick to open up and ramble.

The apparent issue to be discussed in the one-sided conversation was the influx of bears that particular season.

His rant went like this …

"Oh the bears are really getting to me this summer. They're really causing some problems, not just for me, but my wife is so upset about it, she wants to move closer to town.

We have one bear in particular, that drops by our yard every day and comes right onto the deck. And you know what he does? He goes directly to the bird feeder, the one we put up last summer and proceeds to eat the seeds. Well, then the birds get all flustered and start squawkin' and they keep it going from early morning 'til it's time for the nest. I don't know about you but I find as we get older, we need all the sleep we can manage.

The one good thing is it scares the raccoons. Well that's fine with me except those darn raccoons at least keep the mice away and we know how annoying they can be. So, now with the mice dartin' around all over the yard and who knows where in the house, they are nibbling on the lilies for their food.

And that really upsets the rabbits because that's what they eat. So now the rabbits are so out of whack they keep leaving their turd buds all over the deck. It's so darn bad, my wife won't let the grandkids go out there and play. That means they're running wild in our house driving us both crazy. And to top it off, my wife is so damn scared of seeing that bear, she won't go out to hang the clothes … which means using more G*d damn electricity. All because of the G*d damn bear."

As I listened intently I realized that's exactly what happens to us in our lives in the presence of one nagging, growling and irritable person. They kick start the downward spin of destruction. Although too easy to blame the bear, that's when it's time to trap them … divert their attention and send them fleeing in the other direction.

Then kick back and enjoy the peace.

Please Watch Your Step

On a recent trip to Florida, my three girlfriends and I went to a restaurant for dinner. Upon entering we were greeted with two signs. One was: Please Wait to Be Seated. The other was typed out and taped to the hostess desk. It was placed directly at eye level to ensure every guest read it.

DUE TO OUR NEW INSURANCE POLICY,

SENIORS ARE **STRONGLY DISCOURAGED**

FROM SITTING IN THE

UPPER LEVEL BOOTH AREA.

THANK YOU!!

As we each scanned the sign, we in turn burst out laughing with comments like, "Are you kidding me?" "I don't get it. That's discrimination!" "Why would they post such a thing?" "Great, that's what we have to look forward to?" "Is this for real?"

We found it so intriguing we had to ask the hostess why they felt the need to post it.

With a deadpan expression and monotone voice she explained, "You'd be surprised how many of them fall."

We were still giggling as she led us to our table. Once at our places, we turned around to see that all of the seats in the upper level (one step up) were full with patrons. We were quick to notice some of them were seniors. We assumed they either did not read the sign, were not asked for ID, or had boldly accepted the challenge to use at their own risk.

Though the piano player had a limited repertoire and the decor was dated (to a point we shared numerous suggestions for redecorating), the meal was delicious.

As we prepared to pay the bill, we suddenly heard a thud, a roar of voices, and the piano player's yell of: "Oh John! Are you okay?"

With a quick swivel of our heads, we caught what the commotion was all about. John had fallen backwards off the step from the upper level. There he lay sprawled out on the floor as his friends leapt to retrieve him. While the small crowd hovered above him, the piano player stretched her neck in his direction uttering reassurances, all while not missing a beat on the keys.

The hostess gave a quick glance to make sure he was still breathing. And then with a heavy sigh, she uttered a few, "Tsks" under her breath. She immediately rolled her eyes and shot us a defiant look that screamed, "See. I told ya. Now we just have to hope there's no lawsuit."

We left, taking care to watch our step.

Wanna Buy A Red Nose?

When the kids were little we always bundled them up to watch the Oakville Santa Claus Parade. One year as I watched from the curb, I fondly recalled that one of my all time favourite days was when I was a clown in a parade in high school. The wheels were in motion and a plan was hatched.

The next year, I entered *A Fun Group of Family and Friends from Falgarwood* as strolling clowns in the parade. I invited others to join us. We did that for a few years with a whack of kids in tow.

Getting them dressed was always a chore. The day always had a stressful start with assorted wardrobe changes and make-up application for the five of us. It was then a mad dash to claim our spots in the assembly area of the route. Frequently, as we sped to get there, we issued threats of, "Knock off all the whining. Leave that wig on." And the final order, "Just cut it out, we're gonna have fun." Whether they wanted to or not, we usually did.

By 1995, after a few years of walking, waving and the occasional humourous interlude along the route, I thought it might be best to follow the lead of Sunnybrook Hospital. They sold red noses in the Toronto parade as a fundraiser. I immediately researched the idea and my friend Dianne agreed to work with me to execute the plan.

We're proud to say that since then, our group has successfully sold the red noses along the route and have donated well over $50,000 to different local charities. We've had the help of many friends, family members and neighbours over the years and continue to see it as an adventure. Here are a few:

One year, our order of 2,500 noses arrived after negotiating a great price, substantially lower from the year before. Unfortunately when they arrived, they were pink, not red. Dianne and I commiserated about the scam, but ended our rant with a convincing, "Ah, let's forget about it. No one will even notice."

On parade day, as soon as we parked the car and set out on foot, an eager buyer approached us with his family of kids trailing behind. Our first customer. We were ready for a great morning of selling. He took one look at the noses we were handing over and put his hand up, "Stop. Those noses are pink. Forget it. Cancel that order."

Another time, my friend Joanne and I were all decked to the eyelashes in clown attire. We pulled into a parking spot along the street and sat there debating whether it was the best spot to leave the car. As we talked, a man walked up to the car and tapped on the window. I rolled it down. He looked in and earnestly said, "Are you here to watch the parade?" Through our red noses (which he obviously had overlooked) and from behind our oversized glasses, we snorted and mumbled, "No, we're out for a day of shopping."

Ignoring our attempt to lighten him up a bit, he continued, "You know you can be fined for idling. I'm a bylaw officer in another municipality and thought I'd just give you the heads up."

"Well thanks very much for the update. Enjoy your day."

We can never predict what might happen each year. We have challenged vendors selling their wares illegally only to be threatened in return; bands have plowed through us: and way too many times we have been recognized through our makeup despite our attempts at camouflage.

The most memorable year though was 1996. Our chosen recipient was Halton Women's Place and we had successfully collected $2,200 for them. We decided that year, that rather than hand over the cash to be thrown into a pot, we would purchase items from their *wish list*.

So off we went shopping. The last item to purchase was a TV/VCR unit. We had seen it at Costco and were prepared to buy it the next day with the rest of our funds, before delivering the stash.

That night I dropped by sister's place to visit. On the way out, I noticed a box containing a brand new TV/VCR by the door. I asked her about it.

"Is that a new TV/VCR?"

"Yeah, Richard got it from a supplier."

"Oh, I have to buy one as part of our donation to Halton Women's Place. Want to sell it to me?"

She brushed off the suggestion, "Just take it. It's been sitting here for days and I'm sick of tripping over it. We certainly don't need it."

"Are you sure? I have the money and would gladly buy it from you."

"No, just take it. I'll be happy to have it out of the hallway."

Hmm, great deal. I packed it into the van and headed home.

The next morning feeling unsettled about not paying for it, I called her and once again asked, "I don't feel right about taking the TV. How much do you want for it? Really, I have the money for it."

She said, " OK, hold on. I'll go ask Richard."

I could hear her as she yelled out to Richard who was upstairs, still sleeping. "Richard, Sooze (a family nickname) wants to know how much for the TV." No answer from him. Again she tried. "How much do you want for the TV?"

After a few more ill-fated attempts at getting a response from him, she returned to me and said, "Fine. How about $100?"

I agreed and promised to drop the money off later.

That afternoon, Joe spoke with Richard. When he got off

the phone he informed me that Richard was annoyed at Sharon and me. He felt that we went behind his back and struck a deal without asking for his input.

Although I was outraged at his misperception I did feel badly about upsetting him. I loved him too much to be in his bad books. This had to be dealt with, and right away.

Off we drove back to their place. I had Joe put the box at the front door in the original location. As I went off in search of Richard, I issued a warning to my sister, "Please stay out of this, I'll take care of it."

Finding him in the family room, I announced that I wanted to start over with the TV. I explained the situation and how it had unravelled. I then pointedly asked if he would sell it to me and if so, how much did he want for it. Calmly, he agreed that he'd let me have it and but also that he felt he should have originally had a say about it. I tried presenting our side (the truth), but then thought it best to let it go. He said $200 would be fine.

When my sister overheard this from the other room she screeched, "Are you kidding me? You should give it her." Ignoring the outburst, I went on to explain that if I were to buy it from Costco, I'd be paying $375 plus tax, so I handed over $300 to settle it. A handshake and a hug and back it went into the van.

Updating Dianne on the acquisition, we agreed to arrange the delivery to Halton Women's Place for Monday morning. Rather than move the box yet again, I decided to just leave it in the van. We continued to drive around with it all weekend.

On Sunday, we went to a family Christmas party held at a church in Hamilton. After a night of too much of everything, we packed up and went out to load the van with stuff and kids. To our surprise, there was no van to be found. It was gone. Our family vehicle, which we wanted to drive off a bridge anyway, was finally out of our life. It had been stolen. As we stood there bewildered and wondering what to do next, I mentally reviewed all that was in it: the tapes, the books, the cell phone that was as big as my head and oh we can't forget my favourite blankie. And then it hit me. I screamed, "OH NO, THE TV WAS IN THE BACK!!"

The next day after dealing with the police, the insurance company and telling the family what had transpired, I met with Dianne to discuss the theft of the TV. Hmmm, the details of our donation had already been announced, the money was all spent and now we had no TV/VCR to show. My brother suggested that maybe we could get some newspaper coverage on it. Since it was close to Christmas, they might be able to do something for us. We agreed it sounded like a good idea. I called the paper to set it up.

That night in the middle of my restless sleep, I bolted up with a troubling thought. If they ask me where I got the TV and I say from my brother-in-law, it may read like it *fell off a truck* and I couldn't dare risk tainting his reputation.

The next morning I woke up feeling very nervous and unsettled about the whole thing. I wasn't looking forward to hearing back from the paper. I didn't know how I could deflect their inevitable question: "Where did you get the TV?"

Before hearing from the paper, I got a call from Danny our insurance man. He had some good news for me. He explained that when the insurance company heard our story, they agreed to cover the cost of replacing the stolen TV. What a relief.

When the paper finally contacted me for the interview, I shared the good news with them about the replacement TV. They were pleased about the way the story had unfolded. It would be a great Christmas story for them.

A lengthy article was then written and printed in the Christmas Eve edition of the *Oakville Beaver*. There was no mention of where the original TV/VCR came from. Phew!

Years later, we continue with our fundraising efforts with the red noses.

We complete each day of sales with all the clowns meeting for breakfast. That's where the stories are told and the real joy of each experience is shared. Care to join us next year?

The Key to Candle Lighting

A group of us attended Mass together prior to our daughters' final basketball game. At the end of Mass we decided to light a few candles ... for reasons beyond winning the game.

There was a display of 50 votive candles arranged beneath a statue. Such candles are generally lit followed by a prayer offering. Unlike most candles, these were electric, therefore activated only by a metal wand to complete the circuit. The sign read: *VOTIVE CANDLES $2.*

Helena was the first to put her cash into the metal box. She had dropped in $5, hoping to light three candles. By the time we nestled up beside her with our own coins, she was still struggling with the wand. They weren't lighting. Fearing a waste of money and that perhaps *the message would not be sent* we started fiddling with a few of them to determine what the issue might be.

Just then an older Italian woman (takes one to know one) seeing our struggle came to join us at the display. She motioned with a wag of her gnarled fingers, "Stoppa, no mora." She dug into her purse and pulled out a key. Helena mentioned she had put in $5 but it wasn't working. There were a few more *stoppas* declared as she proceeded to jiggle the key through the slot.

We joked that she must be the keeper of the candles because after all she had the key. As she wiggled it back and forth, in broken English she, "No needa money ... justa lighta da candle."

Helena did as directed and lit her three candles ... at her self determined bargain rate of 3/$5. Again the woman slid in the key and again the candles were primed for Reta and I to light. And again she reminded us, "No needa money, justa lighta."

We wondered why she wasn't encouraging payment when she was the key holder ... but then we realized that the key she was using had nothing to do with the display. It was her house key. (Hmm, how exactly did she do that? And what made her think to do that?)

We figured she had been offering up her prayer offerings free for years and was quick to share her hospitable nature with others. No wonder the sermon that day was about a major fundraising effort to offset a financial shortfall at the church.

Some Perspective ...

For many years Joe and I volunteered at a local Christmas dinner for 2,000 of the city's underprivileged. When Dante was 16, I thought it would be good for him to experience the event in hopes to broaden his perspective.

After the guests enjoyed their dinner they visited an area called the Christmas Store where they traded their ticket for an age appropriate gift. For the children, this was of course the highlight of the day.

Dante and I were placed together at the gift table for girls ages five to seven. We spent the afternoon unloading boxes of board games, dolls and stuffed animals and displayed them in the most inviting manner for the young shoppers. We had fun with each child as they perused the table in search of the perfect gift. Every one left elated.

One young girl approached the table with the look of excited anticipation. Nervously she bit down on her bottom lip as she squeezed her ticket and rolled it between her fingers. While she studied each gift from one end of the table to the other she didn't talk or touch. It was an important decision and she was taking it seriously.

As our only customer at that moment she had our undivided attention. We gradually showed her the entire selection of gifts. She paused in front of a Beanie Baby and petted it; then she reached out for the Barbie and smoothed her hair; next she opened the board game and spun the spinner.

Her mother was waiting behind her, draped over a stroller with a toddler and another child at her side. She looked a little haggard and a lot impatient. She huffed, pushed the stroller into the back legs of the young shopper and growled, "Take the Barbie."

The little girl was not convinced. She reluctantly picked up the Barbie, then went back to the Beanie Baby. More hesitation followed. Dante and I continued to be at her service. Once again the mom nudged her with the stroller. Louder, this time she snapped, "JUST TAKE the Barbie."

But again the child waffled from one gift to another. Her indecisiveness appeared to be as painful to her as to her mom, growing annoyed and restless in the background.

Finally her mom had had enough. She rammed the stroller into her legs a third time and demanded, "JUST TAKE THE F**KING BARBIE."

I leaned over the table and quietly spoke to the little girl. "Honey. I think your mom wants you to take the Barbie."

With tears in her eyes, she bobbed her head, handed over the worn and wrinkled ticket, picked up the Barbie and turned away.

Thankfully we got busy with other eager shoppers so we had little opportunity to discuss the incident. But that didn't mean we forgot about it.

Hours later, on the way home, I asked Dante what he thought of his day of volunteering.

All he said was, "Geez, after seeing that mom, you look really good."

Maybe it wasn't exactly the perspective I had anticipated, but it was a lesson.

Releasing the Cord

As parents we frequently hear the call to *cut the cord*, which implies the letting go of your child from your grasp.

I always pictured mine as a bungee cord with each child tightly gripping one end as I squeezed the other. Gradually the length of the cord would stretch according to their growth. The distance of the cord extended as the parameters of personal safety were set for them – from our arms and crib – to a confined floor area – to playroom – to backyard – to front yard – to your own street – to nearby park – to school and so on and so on and scooby dooby doo on (sorry I had to add that).

As that cord lengthened they spent more time away from us, their anchor, than with us. We spent most of that time tugging to pull them back as they yanked their way to freedom. But they always knew they were still attached and could and would return to the safety nest of their home at a mere turn.

And then in a blink, it's time for them to leave the nest 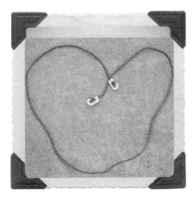 and release the cord (careful it doesn't snap back and hurt you). They leave their home, where we spent half a lifetime tending to them, nurturing them and providing for them. Off they go to do it on their own at school, travelling or pursuing their career. (Don't worry, although the grip on the cord is gone, instinctively they know it's still there to reach for as needed.)

For some of us this break causes that dull ache that weakens our heart and lingers in our bellies. We yearn for the way it was, whether good or bad because it's familiar, it's comforting and it's ours. We hold our loose end of the cord with mixed emotion. However while many of us cry and bemoan the fact they're no longer under our wing, there are others who gleefully pop the cork of the champagne in celebration. (I admit I was that mom when they returned to school each fall.)

For the first few days we might retreat to where they were, organize their empty space (void of their body, not of their stuff) and purge what was mistakenly left behind. Somehow it brings us comfort. At least until we discover *what* was left behind.

Then when we stop busying ourselves up we both wonder and worry about them. "Are they settled? Are they safe? Are they OK?"

Next is the assessment of our parenting: "Did I prepare them enough? Did I relay the essentials? Did I say everything I wanted and needed to before they left?"

And while we twitch in the discomfort of their absence we ignore what we still have … our life, albeit altered from its most recent state. If we have a partner it forces us to pull back and refocus on what it was that brought us together in the first place. It becomes the stage in our relationship when we question, "Hmm, how do we even begin to resurrect this?"

So maybe it's time to get reacquainted with the former *you* that existed pre-kids, before you were best known as 'Sara's mom or dad.' Yep we used to have a *life* and now is the time to do a recall on it and try to remember what we did for fun; what got our heart racing; and what we loved to do but had no time for, whether related to career, friendships or other passions.

At the same time now that your hands are free you might use this period as an opportunity to tweak the nest because before you know it the front door will again fly open to the roar of, "We're back!" … emphasis on *we* because chances are they will be accompanied by someone else or some-thing. (Or you can always sell the house and forget to send the change of address card.)

*Segue: In 2009 Joe and I experienced a shortened period (our one and only) of empty nesting and had gradually developed a new groove of existence. Then Dante the firstborn returned from living out west and as he entered our home left a wave of destruction along his path from curb to kitchen and beyond. Vince soon followed toting a truckload of *ebay* purchases of size 14 shoes. And soon after Alena came home armed with eight months worth of memories and mementos from her year at prep school.. But wait. Then my 89 year old mom moved in to convalesce in our home of hope, healing and humour. The nest was empty for so short a time I don't think I even got a chance to vacuum. *Segue Ends*

And although as parents we always welcome our kids back with open arms we will inevitably again pine for the way it was as an empty nester … *sans* kids, *sans* shoes and *sans* the chaos.

So really all we can do is enjoy each stage as it is presented, make the necessary adjustment and be thankful for each one. But I wouldn't throw away the bungee cord just yet. You never know when and how you might use it again. Besides my kids just don't seem to want to *let go* … I blame Joe.

Not again …

When we bought our first SUV, with so much money invested, I expected perfection. I diligently made a list of ailments for the first checkup (funny but I did this with my babies too). High on the list I noted an incessant 'wind noise' echoing through my vehicle when traveling over fifty.

Of course when I brought it in, they couldn't hear anything (like your cough that suddenly vanishes when you finally get the doctor's appointment). My complaints continued. The noise was driving me crazy … and I was driving Joe crazy. The service technicians did little to correct the problem or to pacify me. Finally one customer service rep flippantly suggested, "Play your music louder." I scowled at him and vowed my determination to continue the fight.

Coincidentally when I returned home that day, a letter had arrived from Head Office, with the message: "We want to hear from you … our valued customer." I couldn't respond fast enough. I immediately pounded out a letter to the president himself. He obviously didn't really want to hear from me because all I received in return was, "*Blah, blah, blah,* we hope you continue to enjoy your vehicle."

With letter in hand, I then met with a service manager at another dealership to share my outrage and ongoing concerns. He was perfect for me as he listened, acknowledged that there indeed was a wind noise and outlined a plan of attack to get to the bottom of the problem. Immediately I felt better.

Over the next few months, the service crew closely investigated the sun roof, side window moulding and the windshield trim, all to no avail.

I eventually had to accept that the noise was never going to go away. I had lost the fight. I thanked him for his efforts and begged myself to forgive and forget. Amazingly, I managed to do just that for the next nine years of the life of the car.

The replacement vehicle was purchased last summer. All imperfections were identified for the first check-up and corrected to my satisfaction.

However, on a recent road trip I was disturbed to suddenly hear that eerily similar wind noise as we travelled along the highway. I scoured the seams of the interior in silence searching for the air leak. Stumped, I brought my new beef to Joe's attention. An all too familiar and impassioned rant followed. He shot me that look that screamed, "Please, not again!"

I sighed heavily and turned up the radio.

Drip Coffee? No Thanks!!

I was invited to a meeting with a group of women I didn't know, in an upscale part of town. I arrived early so I had a chance to chat with the host before the others arrived.

She greeted me at the door, welcomed me into her beautiful home and asked if I'd like a cafe latte? I expressed (oops) that that would be great as I hadn't had my morning coffee yet.

As she moved about her kitchen preparing the drink she talked about her recent trip, the upcoming event and that she had been battling a cold. On my best behaviour, I listened intently and patiently waited for my cup of brew.

She announced that it was finally ready, placed a cup of coffee in front of me and positioned herself to pour the whipped milk through the strainer for the final touch.

She had been sniffling. Just as she was about to pour I noticed a clear droplet resting at the tip of her nose. In and out it went with her steady breathing but suddenly she missed an opportunity to inhale. Bent over my cup, pouring the froth, I watched the drip   slowly   leave   the   tip   of   her nose   and   fall   … as if in slow motion.

Seeming longer than it was (not the drip) I watched in anticipation of its landing. In the length of time it took to drop, I speed dialed my thoughts for my emergency plan. This was clearly a question suitable for the Scruples game. WHAT WILL I DO??????

Thankfully no action was necessary as it missed the cup and landed on the floor thus avoiding any embarrassment.

She appeared oblivious. I contained my relief.

My Dad the Inventor

My Dad was meant to be an engineer. Life circumstances interfered so instead he spent his spare time doing creative home repairs, tinkering and scheming to develop new gadgets. They ran the gamut and included such notables as a fireplace attachment to direct the hot air, golf ball retriever to drag through ponds and a curling stick for aging curlers.

One day (circa 1970) I asked if he was working on anything interesting. He proudly announced, "Yeah, a garage door *closer*. Come outside and I'll show you."

We went outside and manually opened the heavy metal garage door. He tossed me his keys and directed me to get into his car. He then handed me a small block of wood.

"What's this for?"

Irritated by my lack of confidence, he griped, "Just hold onto it and back up." I obeyed.

As I reversed out of the garage an interesting thing happened. The small block of wood I gripped was attached to a wire, measured perfectly so as the car reversed, the wire slowly tugged on the heavy metal door. By the time I edged onto the driveway, the door shut closed in front of me and the block of wood was pulled from my hand.

Hmm, pretty good. I was impressed. It was an ingenious start. But before he could invent the *opener,* we gave him a real one for Christmas. I detected his disappointment.

Patient Confidentiality?

My doctor suggested I book an appointment for a mammogram.

Fearing the dreaded 'outreach for one of my loosely hanging appendages by the technician who is trained to avoid eye contact and has just iced her hands, to then place what she grabs between a metal vice to squeeze until my ears pop'... I reluctantly called our local clinic to make an appointment.

The person who answered the phone had a doddering tone. As well, she had difficulty hearing what I was saying and spoke considerably louder than was necessary. I knew the layout of the clinic. Surely anyone in the waiting room could hear her every word.

Our conversation went like this:

"Medical Clinic. How may I help you?"

"Hi. I'd like to make an appointment for a mammogram."

"A mammogram? Sure. And what is your name?"

"My name is Carole Bertuzzi." I deliberately chose to omit Luciani for simplicity.

"You said it was Carole? Would that be with or without an '*e*'?"

"That's with an '*e*'."

"So that's *C-a-r-o-l-e*?"

"Yes that's right. And my last name is Bertuzzi."

"BERTUZZI? Oh dear. You're going to have to spell that one."

With each reply, her voice got louder and I envisioned the crowd in the waiting room raising their eyebrows over their tattered magazines.

"Yes that's right. *B-e-r*"

"*B-e-r.*"

"*T-u.*"

"*T-u.*"

"*Z-z-i.*"

"*Z-z-i.* Oh yes, I see. So that's BERTUZZI ... *B-e-r-t-u-z-z-i?*"

"Yes"

"And, so you're Carole Bertuzzi and you'd like to book a mammogram?"

"Yes please."

"Hmm, CAROLE BERTUZZI. Are you the one with the breast implants?"

"Ah, no. I am NOT. Now can you please announce that for everyone listening in your waiting room to hear?"

Hairdresser Dating

I've had more *hairdresser relationships* than I have had romantic ones … or at least they have been more memorable. And unfortunately for every relationship with the holder of the scissors, there has been a breakup.

My needs have changed over the years as have my hairstyles, no matter how minute the alteration. Though forever short, the look has varied depending on the rage from *Twiggy* length to long-short; bangs low, bangs high; long wispy sides; hair spiked, gelled out, swept to the side or dippity-dooed.

My hairdresser dating goes back to when I was 4 years old. That bond lasted six years. I just didn't know how to end it. He made me squirm in the chair which led to years of *Buster Brown haircuts* … with crooked bangs. The trust just wasn't there.

Next was a connection my mother encouraged … with the son of her own Italian stylist. But he showed no respect for me or my wish to have *Beatle bangs*. It just didn't work out.

One of my most successful bonds was with a hunk named Malcolm, newly transplanted from England. We dated right through high school. After graduation, I sadly outgrew him.

Some were one-night stands never to be seen again. Some were vacation romances as I looked for something more exotic, but typically the new look only lasted until the first washing. Then there was the one who had different preferences. He was actually a barber, hence my short lived buzz cut.

Lots of casual dating took place with service provided by those with names I can't remember. I was fickle. If they owned a pair of scissors and I'd save $10, I was at their mercy. Besides, I would rationalize that it only takes two weeks to grow out a bad cut.

I dated Dominic out of convenience as he was close to my work. It lasted many years. When the job ended, we broke up more than once but I kept going back for more. In the end I couldn't cope with the long distance relationship.

One was abusive. I sat on eggshells not knowing what mood he might be in. Once when I asked about the length of one of my *sides* he scowled at me in the mirror, stepped around the chair to face me and snapped, "You want the f***king scissors?" I purposely kept my mouth shut, because he still had the scissors. I feared leaving the shop looking like I'd gone through a Magic Bullet. I never returned.

I endured more than a few set ups when some third party figured we'd be good together. But after a couple of dates in the chair, things got boring. One set-up was local. I dare not look inside that shop as I pass, for fear we might make eye contact.

My most recent relationship began after going to the dentist (like my mother always said, "You could meet the *right one* in church" … so why not at the dentist). After I returned home the receptionist called to say there was a patient in the waiting room who was a hairdresser. He had asked about me. Apparently he yearned to get his hands on my hair. I surprised him and showed up for an appointment. What started as a blind date now continues to flourish in an open relationship.

He lets me be me. He gives me my space. We can go months and not see each other. He's there for me as I grow thick and my hair grows thin. He listens. I trust him and he trusts me. He knows I'm not seeing anyone else. He knows I'm just spending more time on my own ... cutting my own hair. And no matter how much I screw up, he always takes me back. His name is Cecil (BeBop Hair). Don't tell Joe.

Please, Don't Touch the Melon

*Y*ears ago, I had two medical procedures done within a short time.

One day as I was walking through the produce section of our local grocery store, I met up with someone from the neighborhood who was shopping with a friend. As we chatted, she expressed concern about my recent knee surgery and asked if it was OK if she and her friend could pray over it. It wasn't something I would normally encourage, but who am I to judge? I shrugged my shoulders with an uncertain, "Sure."

They proceeded to place their hands on my knee with bowed heads and closed eyes. In unison they recited their prayer of healing as I stood like a pelican on one leg, scanning the interior of the store.

As I tried to appear unfazed by this public display of intimacy, I sheepishly thanked them and continued shopping.

All I could think of was thank goodness they hadn't heard about my lumpectomy procedure.

Drama 101 … Exit Stage Left

Early on in my career as a professional speaker, I welcomed opportunities to enhance my skills. I scoured old issues of Toastmaster magazines looking for tips, studied TV evangelists for their impact on their congregations and even enrolled in a clowning course to help with the use of props. I was hungry for info and ready to learn.

In 1989, when the boys were three and two and I was pregnant with our third, a pamphlet came my way. It promoted a week long acting program presented by a group of experienced drama coaches from the area. The workshop *Drama 101* caught my eye. I read the course content with interest. I don't know whether it was the possibility of broadening my skills as a speaker, or the fact that I could be away from Joe and the boys for one whole week, but I was definitely interested enough to register.

Mid July, I travelled to Trent University for my seven-day trip into the acting world. Prior to that, my only theatrical experience was a 27 second role of comedic relief in a high school production of *David and Lisa*. Not much of a bio, but surely I would not be the only neophyte enrolled.

With some trepidation I headed towards the registration area to check-in. I was calm as they handed me my package outlining the daily agendas. Inside, among the papers was my room key. Casually asking if it was the only key to the room, I was advised that it was a single room and yes, it did have a washroom. That's when I got really excited. My own room and my own toilet. One whole week of privacy and now I couldn't wait for it to begin.

I unpacked and created a nest for myself. When I had things organized, I studied the schedule and materials. First on the itinerary was a *meet and greet* that evening in the seminar room. It was an opportunity for registrants of each class to gather, introduce themselves and enjoy some refreshments. That didn't scare me. I am a schmoozer and I always enjoyed meeting new people.

In preparation, I sifted through my limited maternity wardrobe to find something suitable that I'd feel good in. With just minutes to spare, I headed down to the room.

Before I entered, I peeked through the doorway for an early glimpse of the group I'd be sharing my week with. Whoa, it was definitely a collection of theatrical types. You know them. You've seen them. You've watched them in awe. When these people get dressed in the morning, they don't just throw on something that fits and is comfortable. Oh no, they go for the wow factor. They are the ones who can stroll down Main Street wearing the big turquoise felt fedora. They're the ones who can carry off wearing a six-foot scarf draped over their left shoulder and it doesn't move an inch all day. When they walk into a room, they don't just shuffle in. They swing, they sway and they skip into that room. And when it's time to introduce themselves, they don't just mumble their names in monotone. Oh no. They do it in rap, they do it in rhyme or they do it in song.

Looking through that doorway, I started to feel intimidated. Suddenly a suppressed shyness came over me like a veil and I found myself retreating into a shell I didn't know I had. Stepping back, I closed my eyes and took a deep breath before being sucked into the room by the energy that filled it. I mustered the courage to introduce myself and chat with my fellow classmates. I managed to survive the night but phew, it was a challenge.

The next morning we met for our first workshop. Our instructor introduced himself in theatrical style, but all eyes were on his very very short shorts. I'm sure I was not the only one in the room who was wondering what, exactly, he had done with all those body parts.

He began his lesson with a few creativity-enhancing exercises. Being a recreation and camp-type person, I was used to ice breaking exercises that were fun and light-hearted, but nothing in my experience had prepared me for what was to come. Every exercise he led us through was painful for me and I found myself wrestling with foreign feelings produced by his instructions to really *let it go.*

By Tuesday night, I was exhausted. I had doubts that I was cut out for this new experience and oh yeah, Joe and the boys .... well, let's just say I was really missing them.

Grappling with my concerns about this out-of-my-comfort-zone experience, I decided what I needed was to psych myself up. With pointer finger directed back into my own face, I exhorted, "C'mon, you can do this, Carole. Tomorrow I want you to go back in there with renewed interest. Be open to this experience, welcome the awkwardness of it and embrace it as yours." And with one final jab, "Besides, you paid big bucks for this so go out and get your money's worth." Sighing, I promised myself that I would.

The next morning I entered the class feeling refreshed. I was ready for whatever directives the teacher issued. His first instruction was, "I ask you all to please stand." I did, and with a smile on my face. I was determined to follow through and enjoy each of the steps.

Next, he said, "Now please close your eyes." So far so good, I thought. Hang in there; you can do this.

At his final instruction, "I want you to imagine ..." my new-found determination had evaporated. I felt the stirrings of panic. The last time I was part of a group when I was asked to imagine something, it turned into an out of mind experience with me doing ridiculous things on stage for the entertainment of a large audience. Nevertheless, I silenced my fears enough to listen for the rest of the instruction.

"I want you to imagine that your world is a bubble. Feel your world growing; feel your mind expanding; where is the window and where is the door?"

All I could think was, where is that door? Get me outta here!

"I want you to stretch the walls of your bubble. Release your strength from within and push it out into the world."

Yikes, thank goodness my friends aren't here to see me now.

As I obligingly flailed my arms in an outward motion within my imaginary bubble, I made a new decision. In order to continue I would have to be true to myself and satisfy my fears about looking foolish. To do this, a slight modification of the procedure was required. I would have to open one eye.

Feeling immediate relief, I carried on with the exercise while furtively checking the room with my open eye. And, I couldn't believe what I saw. Surrounding me in that tiny conference room were all of my creative colleagues, each performing the task with one eye open too.

It comforted me to know I wasn't the only one feeling a little self conscious and hesitant to *let it all go* because I realized that we all share the same fear. No one wants to look foolish.

I'm not convinced that the workshop succeeded in enhancing my public speaking, however that one lesson was worth the price of registration.

Elevator Eavesdropping

On a family trip to Myrtle Beach, our break coincided with a state cheerleading competition. Everywhere we went there were hordes of young girls with identical hairstyles decorated with weaving coloured ribbons high on their head. They had similar lean and athletic bodies that they proudly strutted around the resort and were not shy to entertain us with their backward flips down the hallways. You knew which ones made up a team with their matching attire and similarly adorned moms in the shadows … even their minivans roared with team spirit.

They were everywhere. In every open space of the property you could see them practise their routines and hear them shout their cheers. Their presence provided easy fodder for our conversations.

One day Alena entered our suite and announced, "A funny thing just happened." And she proceeded to tell us about the most recent sighting.

She was on the elevator with some young girls and a few moms. As the young girls exited and the doors closed one mom said to the other in her southern drawl:

"Did you see those cu-ute shorts they were wearing with CHEER on the butt? We should see if we can get a pair."

"Ye-es I did. But I doubt if I could get a pair to fit. My butt's soo bi-ig, it would have to say CHEER-LEADER."

Rookie Mom's Jitters

Before we had children, Joe and I made an agreement. Our lives would not revolve solely around our kids. We agreed that they would fit right into our lifestyle and easily join us in our family's journey through life. It sounded like a good plan.

My life changed the day Dante was born. I no longer enjoyed the element of control I was used to having. Suddenly my schedule was based on his life rather than mine.

Although he arrived in no particular hurry, two weeks later than scheduled, Dante lived according to the hands of the clock during his hospital stay. Precisely every four hours, his wailing blasted through the silence of the nursery. The nurses would bundle him cozily up in a cotton blanket and present him to me like a beautifully wrapped package. As I fed him his bottle, or more accurately as he inhaled its contents, I would feast on the smell of his skin. I'd nibble on his ear lobes, sniff every pore and kiss every available part of him. I was falling in love. (Note: Dante was apparently the only baby in Canada who was not being breast-fed at the time. Despite the many warnings that came my way about the negative repercussions of bottle-feeding, he seems to have turned out okay. Phew.)

By the time I was ready to leave the hotel, I mean hospital, the nurse approached me with some sound advice: "You have a good baby here. He's already on a schedule. Don't screw it up!"

Fine, I now had a mission. Set the timers, synchronize the watches; this baby would punch a time clock.

Once home, I was determined not to deviate from his schedule. Every four hours to the minute, like a buzzer had just gone off in his belly he'd let out that unmistakable yowl. I'd heat the bottle and toss it into the open tunnel of his wail. Not three minutes later, he'd have that bottle sucked dry to the plastic liner. He would then unceremoniously let out a burp that resonated off the walls like a clap of thunder before settling contentedly back into a four-hour snooze.

Hey, this wasn't bad. Except that there were 22 hours every day when I would hang around wishing I had something to do. The way I saw it, I was really only needed for about two hours a day, and since I wasn't breast-feeding, anyone could hold the bottle. I could probably just go back to work. When visitors dropped by, they were certainly allowed to peek into his crib but they had strict instructions not to wake him up for fear of ruining the routine. To maintain the schedule I took him for daily walks bundled in the Snuggly. It was so soothing he never woke up.

By day seven, I finally had something of significance on which to focus: the first doctor's appointment. I purposely tried to arrange it for a time when I figured he would be awake and things wouldn't be too disrupted. I flitted around all day getting things ready and organized down to the very last detail. Bath water was set, clothes laid out, diaper bag packed and ready to go in the van with essentials ranging from a day's worth of formula and diapers to the hand-me-down copy of Dr. Spock. The van was gassed up and car seat secured. I even backed the van into the driveway for a quick getaway.

I watched the clock closely, pacing the day away. I had been getting so bored with such low activity days that this trip had become the highlight of my month. The day had been meticulously planned: he would wake up according to schedule, I'd give him his bottle, immediately bathe and dress him, and off we'd go for the first foray outside the neighbourhood. I was in control.

He overslept. I had to wake him. He snoozed as I frantically attempted to carry through with my plans. Strangely enough, despite all the waiting around we were actually running late. A sense of panic came over me. I guess a part of me thought it was important to arrive at the doctor's office in a timely fashion and in a heightened state of preparedness, appearing as though I had made an effortless transition to motherhood.

It was September, and the fall months can be cool, right? I decided to dress him in a velour sweat suit, which happened to be only slightly larger than a Barbie doll outfit. I dug out the knitted sweater and matching hat my aunt had made for him. Then, just in case there was a breeze, I folded him into the bunting bag. As I zipped him tight, I heard the bubbles blowing from his bottom. Nuts! Back to the bare skin again. Wiped, creamed and powdered, I dressed him a second time.

We dashed out to the van, which was waiting for us in the ready position. I secured him in his car seat. Holding soother in place, I fumbled around for the keys. I had left them in the house! Back in I went, locked up and drove off ... very, very carefully. This was my first drive with him; I didn't want to make him nervous or upset that sensitive belly of his. I kept the radio off so as not to startle him.

Maneuvering the vehicle as though on a test drive, I started to sweat. My pores had opened. My jacket weighed heavily on my shoulders. Could it be the carton of wipes I had thrown into my pocket for good measure? Or perhaps the three puppets I had stashed in the other? I checked the temperature gauge in the minivan and it read 23 degrees Celsius. I looked at the beads of perspiration lining Dante's face, but I convinced myself that there was still a cool breeze, and decided not to take any chances with his clothes.

I finally pulled into the parking lot of the doctor's office. I darted around to his side of the car and with diaper bag slung over my shoulder, pockets drooping with weight, I gingerly scooped him up, car seat and all. Hands full, back loaded and soother between my own teeth, I kicked the door shut.

I hustled in as quickly as possible as I was already ten minutes late and I would hate to hold up the doctor from his own important schedule. I entered the waiting room. There was not an available seat. Wow, I thought, there must be an epidemic happening. I finally spotted an empty chair in the corner. Smiling nervously, I half expected these strangers to ooh and ahh over my beautiful baby as I worked my way to the seat. Plunking myself down with car seat on my lap, I started organizing Dante for presentation.

His hair was dripping wet. I slowly unwrapped the many layers that encased him. He started to fidget. I rummaged through the bag for a distraction. Eventually settled, my eyes roamed around the waiting room. Surrounding me on all sides was the most miserable bunch of people I had seen in a very long time. They coughed, they sniffed, they sighed and they squirmed in their seats. It was obvious they had been waiting a long time and had lost their patience.

I started to remove my own jacket. I was soaked too. I turned to the guy beside me who seemed restless from what must have been a bad case of hemorrhoids. When I'm a little nervous I like to chat. I made a feeble attempt with him. "Phew. Sure is hot in here today, eh?"

Arms crossed, with chin to chest he stared down his nose at me. Then, with no trace of amusement in his voice, he growled, "I think you're a little excited."

Oh. I was hoping it wouldn't be so obvious. But embarrassingly, I guess it was.

When I packed up to return home that afternoon, I seemed to have turned the corner on the paranoia of parenthood. I stripped Dante to his undershirt and lowered the windows to enjoy the tail end of a summer breeze. I cranked up my Springsteen tape, and as I rode along the highway, I belted out a laugh so hard it made Dante scream. Ah, no big deal. He'll get over it!

Disturbed by the Storm

I was awakened around 4 a.m., not by the high winds, pounding pellets of rain or the crackling branches of the storm of the century (Frankenstorm). Nope. I woke up to the droning sound of what seemed like human moans or at the very least a dying animal. Although my sound sensors were alert I was not disturbed enough to be really concerned. After all, we have no pets and the basement boarder (our son) is out of my hearing range. I tried to ignore it.

As I listened closer I wondered if those sounds were coming out of both ends of the sleeping body beside me? This required a rollover and upon closer review I realized the usual wheezes, grunts and sighs were gushing from his Darth Vader sleep mask but that was it. The other sound still lingered in the distance.

So what the heck is that noise? Not feeling like investigating further I settled back onto my pillow to try to once again fall asleep.

Moments later I heard Joe get up. Obviously he too had heard the noise which by then sounded like a gurgled and guttural gasp in the distance. Thankfully he went off in search of the annoyance. I'm not good with surprises in the middle of the night and besides I love sleeping so if I'm gonna *go*, I'm *going* in my sleep.

As I followed his steps in my mind I detected exactly where he stopped and aha suddenly realized what he found.

It was the fart machine that sits hidden by the front door (don't ask, but it is within arm's reach of the sign that reads: *Welcome to the Fun House*, and is perfect for when a visitor bends over to tie his shoes ... OK so it has to be the right visitor).

Somehow it had become activated in the night. What we were hearing was a continual roll of various battery-operated farts interfering with our sleep.

The Fartenstorm had struck our household but thankfully all we lost was some sleep.

Lathered in Leather

I went to a designer clothing sale at my friend's house and although most samples were in the size 2 - 6 range, I surprisingly found the most gorgeous pair of oxblood leather leggings to fit. The second best part was they were regularly $660, marked down to $40. I had to buy them. If for nothing else, for the bragging rights to the bargain.

A few days later I decided to wear them. I have no desire to know what animal sacrificed his hide for mine but the leather was buttery soft and felt great on the skin. And they actually looked okay on me, once I accessorized them with the appropriate length top … somewhere just above my kneecaps. As a finishing touch, I put on the perfect chunky jewelry high on my neck to divert all eyes upward. With the outfit coordinated I felt confident in the *look* I had put together.

I sashayed into the family room for Joe's assessment. My son, who happened to be there with him, looked up at me and yelped, "NO. NO. That's wrong." He continued, "That's just not right. Tsk, you are not going out wearing leather pants."

A ping-pong battle between Joe and Dante ensued with Joe heavily favouring his honey. As Dante continued to gag and groan at my outfit he reached for his phone and quickly prepared to snap a pic.

He wanted to share the big laugh on *social media*. I immediately turned away to avoid the flash of fame but he was still able to get a shot of my backside … the butt of his joke.

I bet his *tweet* read … *Mom's affinity to HIDE.*

Some Gifts … Best Left Unused

As I walked through Costco with my mother, she went on a bit of a rant. "You all have too much. You have more stuff than any of you know what to do with."

She sealed it with, "You don't use half of it."

We then passed a display of home fire extinguishers which triggered an example to further support her views.

"Now there's another thing. Just last Christmas I bought you and Sharon and Larry all a fire extinguisher for Christmas. And none of you ever use it."

P.S. When I tell these stories about my mom, please understand I do so with love in my voice … besides, my kids are already sharing their own similar tales about me.

Service with a Sneer

When our Mom was 78, we took her to New York City for a shopping trip. When we got to Macy's she announced she was going to check out the skin care products.

Moments later she returned looking somewhat glum. When we asked her what happened, she told us that she had asked the salesgirl what she would recommend for wrinkles.

From behind the counter, the salesgirl rudely offered, "It's a little late isn't it?"

You Think You Had It Bad ...

There is something cathartic being a part of woeful discussions. We eagerly await an opportunity to play the game of one downsmanship. Oddly it feels good to vent and to share our misfortune with others.

Which leads me to my children, who believed no one had a mom as tough or as strict as theirs ... which means me. They have expressed their feelings by bestowing upon me the title *the strictest mom in Oakville*; they have given me a T-shirt emblazoned with *One Tough Mother* on the back; and have described my mothering style as *parenting like a linebacker*.

No matter how serious their sentiments, I remain proud of their tributes.

One evening, around midnight, the phone rang. Of course it woke me from a sound sleep.

"Mom. It's Vince (like I had forgotten his voice). Can you do me a favor and talk to Andrew. He doesn't believe you sent us to circus school."

Half awake, I groaned, "Okay fine."

"Mrs. Luciani I'm sorry it's so late but I just made a bet with Vince. You didn't really send them to circus school did you?"

"Yep I did. So pay up."

I hung up and rolled over.

As I tried to fall back asleep a few of my other seemingly wrongful acts danced through my mind and I envisioned my kids sitting around together each sharing their own *mother horror stories*. I imagined their opening lines to be: "Ha, you think you had it bad. Let me tell you what she did to me:"

... "She sent me into Tim's with a note to buy her afternoon coffees when I was only three and she made me walk to school by myself when I was just in kindergarten."

... "Oh yeah, well she pulled the plug on my technology just as I was flourishing in my CD burning business and THEN she made me have a liquidation sale of my overstocked closet of precious Jordans."

... "That's nothing. She helped me pack when I told her I was going to run away and I remember she made me finish a gardening job after I was stung by a nest of angry bees ... before taking me to emerg." (ouch)

Each one has assured me there are plenty more examples but there's no need to build too strong a case here.

So I plead guilty. I never did proclaim perfection in parenting. I did and will however, continue to do my best. I just hope at some point forgiveness is granted and my sins will be absolved.

P.S. Thankfully at this point, all three are still talking to me and the *therapy fund* has not yet been tapped.

Wrong Number ... Maybe Not

Growing up we had one phone that rested comfortably in the kitchen of our split level home. For a short time in 1969, our phone number was only one digit off that of the Mississauga Police Department. So numerous times a day one of us had to inform an urgent caller they had dialed the wrong number. After a few weeks of this, it was not only irritating to deal with, but a real pain to traipse up and down the stairs at all hours.

Late one night we were awakened by the phone yet again. There was no question who would take the call. Immediately we heard our dad hot on the trail of the ring, spewing profanities from his bed, down the stairs and into the kitchen. He had been waiting for this opportunity.

We bolted up ... we didn't want to miss any part of our dad's *telephone answering techniques* at the moment.

He shouted into the phone "THIS IS NOT THE G*D DAMN POLICE DEPARTMENT SO I DON'T CARE WHAT YOUR PROBLEM IS."

But before he had a chance to slam the receiver down we heard a slightly more subdued tone drift up the stairs. "You want to speak to Larry? Hold on. I'll see if he's awake." Pounding over to the stairs he yelled, "Larry. Some girl wants to talk to you."

Obviously mortified, we could hear Larry groan as he got out of bed to retrieve the call. What followed, we'll never know. We were too busy smothering ourselves under our pillows, laughing into our sheets.

The Stool … Under Surveillance

On one Junk Week family outing, part of our stash included a vintage stool that was desperately screaming for a makeover. I had an idea for it. It would be a fun addition to the play area in the basement. I had the required supplies collected before the van was unloaded.

I painted the legs black, sprayed the swivel seat gold then painted a fake black NIKE swoosh in the centre … it was the peak of the logo era for my kids (circa 1993, ages four, seven and nine).

Within hours the kids were not only enjoying the swivel action but had made it yet another prop for their play. They were impressed.

A few days later I went downstairs and happened to notice the stool turned over. As I righted its position I was annoyed by what I saw. Across the seat and through the swoosh were a number of prominent scratches. My boiling point had been reached and I screamed for the kids' attention. One by one they fell into line. I got the extension out on my pointer finger and started the inquisition. "Which one of you did this? That is destructive. You ruined a perfectly good paint job. You saw how hard Mommy worked. Who did it?"

I went from face to face, back and forth as I waited for the culprit to confess.

From youngest to oldest I got:

"It wasn't me Mommy. Honest. Do you want me to go to my room?"

"You always think it's me. No fair. I didn't do it."

"Mom don't blame me. It had to be *one of them*."

I couldn't detect a hint of guilt out of any of them.

That night at dinner I hatched a plan. Once the table was cleared I called a family meeting.

My intro went like this ...

"You know I'm very upset about that stool. No one admitted to doing it but you know that's not true. One of you scratched it. It's important that you tell me. So here's what I'm going to do.

I want you all to put your heads down. Whoever did the damage just raise your hand. No one will know but me and Dad. There will be no punishment. I just want you to be honest and admit it."

The three little heads rested on the table with Joe and I anchoring each end. We waited. And we waited. And we waited some more. What started out as mild anger soon became comical. We must have sat there for five minutes waiting for just a glimmer of admission ... but got nothing.

As I bit into my bottom lip to contain my reaction to the scenario, I announced, "OK I now know who did it. You can lift your heads. Thank you for being honest. I just hope it never happens again."

The meeting was over and they left to go play.

Joe and I looked at each other, shrugged our shoulders and agreed it would forever remain a mystery.

Just this past summer the incident came up in conversation. After enjoying a laugh about it, one of the kids finally admitted to the destructive behaviour and to the lie.

I had to forgive. It's what I promised 18 years ago. The other two demanded an apology for the psychological pain they had endured. I'm certain it will be resolved in therapy.

The stool is now under new ownership as it was put out for junk at our own curb years ago.

Surely, We Made His Day

I once shared a small work space of three offices. My coworkers included a demure older woman who was the secretary and a distinguished retired gentleman who, although a volunteer, oversaw our work. We both highly respected him and kept ourselves in check in his company. I, especially, had to tone down my behaviour.

One day, a friend from another department dropped by to retrieve a document. Typically we took advantage of such opportunities to share a quick story and enjoy a laugh together. That day, since we knew we were alone, the joking among us continued.

We somehow reached the topic of fantasies and each willingly shared a secret pleasure. My coworker shyly revealed her desire for mirrors on the ceiling. Coming from her made it even more entertaining so we erupted in rumbling laughter. As we were *coming down* from the outburst of endorphins we heard what sounded like the clearing of a throat from the next room. We were suddenly silenced as we realized we were not alone.

Although my coworker assumed that she should resign because of the incident, thankfully she rescinded.

I assured her it was probably the most entertained he had been in years and I was certain he would soon be sharing his own version of the story with great delight.

A Memory from The Ex

"B-8!" rang out from the caller's microphone. The screeching music from the nearby Ferris wheel filled the air only to be interrupted by false outbursts of, "Bingo!" from the boisterous youths out on the midway. The night was aging and my feet were tiring. The room was a collage of bent heads searching for their numbers through the clouds of haze produced by their incessant puffing of their fags.

I wandered up and down the aisle of my station, content to ignore the harsh orders belted out by the patrons. I would occasionally plant my feet in front of one of the bingo addicts to bring them luck. Anything to distract me from the drudgery of the job. But, I mostly stood and studied the people around me. One pair in particular, got my attention.

Her eyes were as enormous as they were black. The young child was so easy to look at. When she smiled, her white teeth glistened like Chiclets which cast a light on her dark face. The contrast was sharp. Tiny black springs of hair jutted from her scalp into an eye-catching masterpiece. Patiently she sat spinning on the stool beside her father.

Her father, dressed in a dark blue uniform, had the worn look of a man who had worked far too many hours. Deep in thought, his fingers hovered over the page of numbers below. He too was trying his luck at the *fifteen cent each or seven for a dollar* bingo game.

From my view, it appeared the young girl had placed all of her trust in her dad to win her that panda she had been eyeing since they sat down. For the first time in that shift I felt drawn to one of my patrons. As I stood there with a half smile, I closely watched her. With her head tilted forward she peered out at me as her eyes reached for her bangs. Her gaze then travelled to the panda. From the panda she looked to her dad; from her dad to his card; and then to me. She must have thought I could somehow be part of it all.

I stared at the man. He was quiet and calm in his approach to the game. He sat patiently waiting for his numbers to be called. Clearly he wanted to please his little girl with the prize she craved.

In my fascination with the two I tuned out all other cries of "Tickets!", "Change!" And even the occasional "Bingo!" I soon broke the spell. I decided if I couldn't help them win, I could at least buy this young girl an ice-cream cone.

The three of us continued to work together towards those four corners or one line in any direction. I watched the numbers, he watched the card and she watched the panda.

Two dollars spent, 15 minutes gone and the pair got up to leave. Our efforts had failed. They started to walk away but suddenly stopped as the young girl continued to tug at her father's pant leg. A quick glance at me and then to the panda, he flashed an eager smile. From his pocket he pulled a crumpled one dollar bill. I was certain it was his last dollar to spend that night. Without discussion, they decided to stay for one more try. With chocolate ice cream dripping from the corner of her mouth, she excitedly watched as her father carefully placed each chip on his card.

Too soon, that dollar was also gone. And once again they got up to leave. As they walked away, the young girl turned back to offer me one more glimpse of her dazzling smile and to peer one last time at the panda. She then slipped her tiny hand into her father's strong grip and together they stepped into the midway.

Standing there in my aisle I watched them until they were swallowed by the crowd. As my mind drifted further away from the demands of my job and the chaos around me, a dry lump formed in my throat. At that moment I wished I could flee my responsibilities; catch up to the young girl and her father and once again be a part of them. Just the three of us … and the panda.

Yeah, I Win

When our son Dante was in Grade Nine he had a Religion teacher who was a real prankster. It came time for the first quiz of the semester. Dante wasn't a fan of the multiple choice format so when it was time to be tested, he was anxious to get at it and get it over with.

He read through the test and was surprised to notice a bit of motivation typed at the end of it: The first student to finish the test and stand up and shout I LOVE GOD AND GOD LOVES ME will earn 5 bonus marks.

Competitive by nature, he was determined to earn the extra points. He flew through the questions and finished in record time. Before his pencil circled the final 'c' (when in doubt, always choose 'c') he leapt up from his seat and yelled, "I love God and God loves me."

His classmates were stunned. They looked up at him in shock, then collectively burst out laughing at his public display of devotion.

It was only after the laughs subsided that their teacher explained. ONLY Dante had received the notation at the end of the test. Although it was painful to take the ridicule … he was happy to take the marks.

Putting Up the Light Fixture

The following is a actual stream of conversation between Joe and me as we struggled to install a heavy ceiling fixture:

"How are we going to get it up?"

"Well you're going to have to help."

"I think that piece has to be longer."

"Well it's not like we can get an extension."

"You're gonna have to hold it."

"OK I hope not for long because it hurts my arms."

"I'll try to get it in while you keep it in position."

"Is it in yet?"

"No you might have to guide it."

"But I need you higher."

"Why are you sweating?"

"It's been a while since I've worked my arms like this. This is exhausting."

"Good, I think we're done."

"Ahhhhh, thank goodness. My back is killing me. Can I turn the light on now?"

"Yeah, I'll clean up. Let's hope we don't have to do that again for a long time."

I didn't stick around for any congratulatory comments on the great accomplishment. I had to write this down before I forgot it.

At a Loss ... and Losin' It

It bothers me to misplace anything. I'll turn the house upside down in search of the lost and missing and am not against bribing others to find it for me. Then to help me get over it, I picture a nondescript person trudging along the side of the road dragging every one of my lost items with her ... not necessarily in a shopping cart but more like Heidi layered up in various pieces of clothing and adorned with the assorted *found* stuff like a one man band might attach his instruments. And although unrecognizable, her smile is apparent as she relishes in her good fortune.

Some of my favourite misplacements include my 'championship' first base trapper treasured for three decades only to be left behind in the schoolyard by one of my kids. I trust the person enjoying the flapping of that glove is also stepping out in style in my new silver NIKES also forgotten by same offspring (and may they be wearing his two new ski jackets as well) ... but who's keeping track eh?

Just this spring never to be found was our marriage license, my birth certificate and a savings bond. Intruder? No. Forgotten hiding spots? Perhaps. But like most searches for lost articles it does propel me into extreme clean-up mode to organize the clutter. And when all else fails a quick shout out for assistance goes to St. Jude, the patron saint of hopeless causes ... we resort to him over St. Anthony, the ruler of lost things because he's been way too busy lately.

In our gardening business, tools are regularly left behind and inadvertently tossed into piles of debris requiring regular replacement. Short of retrieving my metal detector (I'm actually saving it for the beach when I'm just a bit older) we are not above diving into that brown bag searching for any foreign piece of matter. This may include not just tools, but eyeglasses and jewellery as well.

And don't get me going on single socks and where the heck they land. I can only hope *that* person has used her free time and hands to make a nice cozy and colourful 20' scarf out of them.

But as I mature in body and mind, not to mention years, I believe that perhaps I am as negligent as others in my family as I have noticed more than a few key things transferred into the loss column (Ouch I just remembered that one big financial loss which I will now try really hard to forget).

Recently it has been brought to my attention that I no longer possess a whisper. Yes, that's right. My whispering quiet voice apparently can now be heard by most people within 30' (I am turning into my mother quicker than I had anticipated). My private side-bar conversations must now be kept to a minimum in fear of who might be picking up my audible signals. Pass me the notepad, scribbling it out might be safest. Or maybe a career as a ventriloquist could be next.

Also lost is the quick, ready and automatic retrieval of appropriate words in conversation including the names of my children. So as to keep the chatter going and not interfere with the intended flow of conversation (or story telling) can someone please toss me a name, noun, verb or adjective as I seem to be at a loss here for the one I need. It definitely makes talking more interesting though.

Then there is the loss of my ability to refrain from swearing. That seal was tightly in place for most of my kids' lives but interestingly once it was broken (I believe it was first used on my eldest) it flows so easily and automatically out of my mouth. Truthfully I find it really quite liberating. Just yesterday Joe enlightened me that if I lived in Middleborough MA I could be fined for uttering the *F bomb*. Hmm, that could get expensive.

But truly the most important thing I've somehow left behind is my filter … you know that strainer thing we (I mean those who cook) use to drain the pasta. I have no clue what that word is right now. Picture that thing as the protective layer over our brain that holds us back from saying, sharing or doing something inappropriate. Yeah, well mine has definitely deteriorated. The warranty is up, the guarantee no longer applicable. Perhaps it merely wore out from overuse (a direct result of growing up Catholic, Italian and female). Its pieces have obviously broken away and flushed through the toilet system of my mind.

I now find myself more often than not expressing out loud what I'm thinking … all those thoughts that historically would have been screened, censored and saved for a more private audience or kept to myself forever (no wonder I'm caring extra weight as it surely has been taking up valuable space in me). It could be a reflection of my age or perhaps the influence of my dirty-minded friends but these things are slipping out of my mouth at a rapid rate. And as they do, while I dopily giggle inside, on the outside I display the cringe of, "Oh no. I've done it again."

Conversation is currently like a quick game of word association I am most eager to play:

At the last Santa Claus Parade as I walked the route in full-clown attire selling red noses, I approached a gentleman proudly puffed up in a full length fur coat. In an effort to be friendly, I said, " Wow you must be warm."

He replied "Oh yeah. Pure Canadian Beaver."

Before I could offer him a red nose, I uttered (in what I assumed was a whisper), "Yeah I've got one of those too." Yep, the word beaver points me in a direction not appropriate for young ears. It doesn't help that our local paper has the same name ... oh just try to imagine the fun we have with that one.

Daily my kids say, "Mommmm, really? Did you have to say that?" or "Seriously, what other mother would actually have this conversation with her kids right now?" Or from my own mother as she continues with her lifelong plea of, "Carole now don't go saying anything you're not supposed to." She alternates that request with "Carole can't you just try to be normal?"

The pressure to *behave 'n be good* has been like a straitjacket that I've been slowly wrangling free from for a lifetime.

So yes the floodgates of my messy mind are now opening and all previously screened and guarded thoughts are flowing out of my mouth like hot lava into the gutter of life. But in some bizarre and twisted way, I'm enjoying it.

And that imaginary person I picture toting my every lost belonging ... I'm pretty certain I just saw her off in the distance dragging a long colourful scarf and flapping my trapper baseball glove) in her left hand. And she's wearing some metal thing on her head. Not sure what it's called but it's too bad for her ... because now she's not going to have any fun at all.

Did Anything Good Happen?

$\mathcal{M}$onths before his graduation prom, our son Vince started plotting his plans to get a date. After extending his *asking* deadline numerous times he decided to go with a girl he didn't even know but who told a friend she'd love to be his date. He opted for this selection not because he kept getting turned down, but because he lacked the courage to execute his plan.

Prom night, we sent him off with the usual last minute removal of fluff, tweak of the tie and words of reminder:

"Don't forget to be a gentleman, take lots of pictures and have fun."

Hours later he called us to coordinate the drop off of clothes etc. for the after party. Of course I was anxious to hear about everything …

"Hey, how's it going?"

"It's OK."

"Are you having any fun?"

"Yeah."

"Well you don't sound very excited. How was the meal?"

"Ahh, not very good. Everyone's complaining about it. The chicken was like rubber."

"What about the music? Any good? Are you dancing?"

"Not really. The DJ doesn't seem to have our kind of music. We're pretty much just hanging around."

Now struggling to glean just a smidgeon of positivity out

of our Mr. Happy, I continued ...

"Well, what about your date? Is she enjoying herself?'"

"Hmm, not much. She isn't very happy. She's actually been crying."

"Whaaat? Why?"

"Her dog died today. Her dad just picked her up."

Oh dear. There was no hope. The rose-coloured glasses had fallen off his head.

As I strived to end the conversation on a high note, I was tempted to recite a *mother line* from my own youth ... "Well, did anyone say you looked nice?" I refrained.

P.S. Thankfully, the after party *was a blast ... best night of his life*. I asked no further questions. I didn't need the details.

But, She Does Have Nice Teeth

For most of my life the one distinguishing trait I possessed was *good* teeth. Not only were they healthy, they were perfectly straight (OK, not before my adult teeth grew in).

When I was young, only wealthy people enjoyed such perfection thanks to the *then* status symbol of braces. I had my own system. In between chewing my nails or cuticles I would intermittently use my fingers to squeeze my teeth together in hopes of serving the same purpose as the wired fencing my friends endured. Somehow I believed it worked.

My teeth were white as well, not the whitest on the colour chart but pretty close, especially if I had a tan. An imposing woman once commented on the whiteness, "You have such beautiful white teeth. Do you swallow?" (What's that mean??)

The only time they look the slightest bit off-colour is when I wear clown face makeup … the contrast is not pretty. Fortunately it's not one of my daily makeup applications.

For a young person who was taller than average, carried more weight and was anchored by bigger feet, had smaller eyes and a slightly protruding jaw (there are other flaws but why get into it now?) my teeth were my salvation. I warmed at the mention that I had beautiful teeth. They were my threadbare link to the world of beauty. I gripped that notion tightly. Perhaps that's what caused the clenching.

I wore a mouthguard for sports when no one else considered it; I brushed my teeth after every meal removing residuals that might linger for future savouring; I quickly and proudly presented my best smile for photos. And I continue to obsess about the fear of breaking them. Often, I have to wake myself up from yet another *teeth dream* in which they shatter within my bite. Oh yeah, the analysts could have a field day with me.

Now at 60, my set of 32's (not the ones you're thinking of, they're 38's) are still the same teeth, albeit slightly discoloured from coffee and other diet sins and they remain straight and filled thanks to my brother-in-law, Richard the dentist, who has a supply of Polyfilla within his reach for quick repairs. He has filed down the groove I had created by gnawing at my nails, he has tended to every cavity and generally coached me through ongoing maintenance. But now the one trait that was mine is shared by millions thanks to the world of cosmetic dentistry.

It seems we have now become a society of perfect teeth. If braces weren't worn as a preteen, now that you have some money they're worn at 50. If they are slightly small or chipped, veneers are placed. If the teeth are off a shade on the colour chart, whitening treatment is purchased and applied. If the entire set are just plain bad, a whole new set is installed.

Yep, around the world every image you see of stars, athletes, politicians, newscasters and any public figure is one showing a set of teeth in translucent shades of perfection. In some cases, (I won't name you) your new set includes one or two extra … at least it looks that way as your face appears to be led into the room by your teeth. Picture Mr. Ed (the horse) smiling.

Now with the influx of new treatments, the magnification of our vanity not to mention in some cases having too much money with nowhere to spend it, my one-time beauty trademark has been paled. Now please refrain from sending me emails with reminders: "Oh, but Carole, you have such a pleasant personality" or "But, you're so good with your hands." Please, hold back. Your words mean nothing. I'm OK. Really, I'll be fine. I'll just keep eating to prevent me from grinding away the tension.

On that note I will continue to flash my pearly *off-whites* and maintain my daily practices of teeth care and yes my pre-sleep ritual does include a guard for grinding (a nice touch with my white gloves). Now if I can only do something about that shrill sound I make through the gap in my lower teeth … yeah the one that allows me to whistle *shhhh* with a mere smile.

Vanity in the Algarve

One of the great things about travelling to other countries is learning about the culture and lifestyles of the natives. It's always fun to try and blend into new environments rather than blatantly look like a tourist. Joe and I both enjoyed our two weeks in Portugal.

The trip was in three parts. The first two nights were spent in the city of Lisbon. We toured around the city climbing every hill and walking every sidewalk. On our last evening there, we explored various local bars and restaurants. We capped the late night off with peach nectar schnapps in the hotel lounge. It was a very late night. We partied to the max before heading back to our room a tad tipsy.

We were scheduled to leave for the beach resort of the Algarve at 7:00 a.m. Thankfully, I remembered that our luggage had to be packed and left outside our room by 5:00 a.m. to be loaded on the bus. Beating this deadline by just an hour, we quickly threw everything into the suitcases and pitched them out into the hallway. We made an effort to sober up enough to organize the clothing we would need for the morning. Mission completed, we dropped into the bed.

Two hours later, not yet sober, we were up, showered and making a hasty struggle to dress in time for the departure from the hotel. I looked around for the outfit I had laid out just a few hours before.

"Joe, where's my bra?"

"How am I supposed to know?"

"I told you to be sure not to pack it!"

"Well, don't blame me. You'll have to go without."

"Go without? Are you nuts?"

Gone were the days of letting it all hang out (unfortunately out is now replaced by low) and it had been at least five years since I had sported Band-Aids on my nipples and pranced around in a halter-top. I was not going anywhere without my bra. I let out an exasperated sigh and moped on the bed for as long as I could, hoping that my bra might miraculously appear. Finally, time was up. We had to get that bus.

Reluctantly, I put on my pink fitted polo shirt and let it drape over my shorts. I was not comfortable about this at all. I tried to stretch the shirt out by pulling at the fabric. I slouched forward to create some space for my anatomy to droop. As we headed to the bus, I clutched my purse and placed it close to my chest. No one would catch a peek if I could help it. No eyes would see the nipples. No free show for anyone.

When the bus stopped for a break I didn't want to get out. The driver announced that we would be there for an hour and I realized that I could die of heat stroke if I remained on the bus. So out I skulked.

I ate my ice cream with my arms folded across my chest and hands around the cone as if I was about to bow my head in prayer. My self-conscious behaviour was attracting the attention that I was trying to avoid. Every ten minutes I asked Joe to convince me that no one could see anything. I was starting to irritate him.

We finally arrived at the hotel and hiding behind Joe, I managed to get to the room unnoticed. Finally, I could relax. We got right into our bathing suits and headed to the beach.

Once settled, Joe fell into a deep snooze. I sat comfortably on the towel, absorbing the scenery and studying the people. I suddenly realized that we were on a nude beach. This was intriguing. The bathers looked natural, comfortable and relaxed as they bared it all for the sun. No tugging at the elastic in their suits, no adjusting their tops and not one of them seemed concerned about exposing their body to the world. There was something about it I liked. It appeared to be so liberating. My thoughts wandered and it wasn't long before I was imagining how it would feel to enjoy the warm sun on my entire body. I nudged Joe.

"Joe, give me three good reasons why I shouldn't take my top off right now and sunbathe nude."

Joe bolted up. He strained to take in what I was saying.

"Whaaaat? You want to go nude? After what you put me through this morning? Are you nuts? You're unbelievable!"

Well, although the idea of it was appealing, I decided against the new experience. I was already deeply tanned around my bathing suit and I figured that if I did take my top off, the colour difference would be enough to draw more attention to myself. Unhappily, I spent the rest of the day tugging, making adjustments and flicking sand out of my bathing suit.

I still regret it.

Read the Label

My parents weren't big wine drinkers. One night they were invited to a neighbour's home for dinner. As they went to leave my dad reminded my mom to get a bottle of wine to take.

It wasn't until they returned home that my dad expressed his embarrassment.

"The bottle you chose was the *same one* they gave us when they came here for dinner."

"So? That's okay. That means they like it."

"It was their homemade wine."

Oops.

Worrying ... The Drip of Doom

I remember listening to my mom, aunts and Nona commiserate about all the woe in the world. When they had exhausted the topic and there was nothing more to bemoan they would progress to sharing their personal worries. Somehow in the company of each other they seemed comforted.

As a young person I felt they worried way too much about totally insignificant things. "You're not eating much. What's wrong?" "You look pale. Are you sick?" "When you check into the hotel make sure you check the sheets." It seemed that without expressing worry or concern, they were at a loss for conversation.

Even when we were seemingly enjoying ourselves, laughing and carrying on, one of them would inevitably say, "Go ahead laugh now because soon you'll be crying." Now what the heck is that all about?

Frequently I would respond, "You worry too much. Relax. Tsk, c'mon nothing bad's going to happen." And on I went living my life keeping most of it a secret from them to avoid any further unnecessary worry.

Fast forward many years and here I sit deeply entrenched in parenthood, maturity and menopausal mush. And guess what? All of those little worry genes that possessed my elders have by osmosis now contaminated me. They lie dormant in a rain cloud hovering over my every thought ... involving my kids. It nags me like a constant *drip of doom*.

For example:

One Christmas Vince (middle child) talked about his reading week (why it's called that I'll never know) trip to Cancun with great anticipation.

He was going away with 300 of his closest buddies, if not in real life, at least on *Facebook*. But it seemed that every time he mentioned it, I was quick to remind him about the recent murder, DRIP, shark attack, DRIP, or off-site mugging highlighted in the news, DRIP. I heard myself remind him about safety (in all forms), locking valuables in the safe, wearing sunscreen and yes, to check the sheets in the room for bedbugs. There was just so much to cover. As he filled his suitcase I emptied my dread.

Well Vince left on Sunday. Tuesday night we got a text that he arrived safely ... geez, I didn't realize they were driving there. By Friday I learned that a number of people had heard from him including my mother who said there was something like a "titter message left on her phone" from him. Later Joe came home and said, "I certainly hope Vince isn't using his phone because I just talked to a kid who recently returned from there only to learn he had racked up $3,000 in roaming charges." DRIP. DRIP... "He has no money and I certainly don't have any to bail him out."

Then Dante came upstairs and said, "Hey check this out. Vince got a tattoo" and proceeded to show me a photo of a back with an unattractive thing looking very much like a tattoo imprinted on it. DRIP. DRIP. ... Not only is it ugly but what about the safety of it all ... the shop, the needles. OMG !!!!!!

So to avoid further drenching of doom I went to bed. A few hours later the phone rang and woke me from that *who am I? Where am I* state? Picking it up I noticed part of the name on caller ID read SANTIAGO with a series of obscure numbers listed below. My heart sank. DRIP. DRIP. I answered.

In broken English I heard what sounded like, "Can I speaka with Joya?"

DRIP. DRIP... please tell me this isn't a call from Mexico asking for Joe.

"I'm sorry, who are you looking for?"

"Julia. Isa thisa the Marion Home?"

"Ahhh sorry wrong number."

Vince eventually arrived home ... in one piece. The tattoo was a henna, he assured me it was *feathering* he was doing for his phone use, not *roaming* and although a few did get robbed, he did not. And so far no sign of scratching at bed bug sores.

Once again, lots of wasted time and energy on my part ... worrying. I think it's time I listened to my own advice from my youth: "Relax. You worry too much."

P.S. But I just saw some Facebook pictures. DRIP, DRIP.

I Used to Know That

*M*enopause has a way of playing tricks with my memory. I don't get it. I can recite the entire *Hair* album, can name almost my entire Grade One class and remember the details of most conversations stretching back to high school. But then right out of nowhere the *recall* button (the one that rests mid forehead and requires constant tapping to activate) freezes and my memory screen goes dark.

As I impatiently waited in the car for my son, I urged my daughter to go back in the house to speed him up. The clock was ticking, motor running and I was heating up.

"Alena, go back in the house and tell ... (pause) ... ah tell (a longer pause ensued as I desperately tried to recall his name, running through the list of males in my life; was it Joe, Larry, Richard, David, Andrew?) ... just go in and tell *that boy* to hurry up."

Thankfully, by the time he dropped into the backseat and I caught a glimpse of him through the rearview mirror I remembered. Oh yeah, it's DANTE.

The bruise on my forehead faded after a few days.

Muffie's Coffee Shop

Although I'm uncertain of the exact lineage of the restaurant, I do know it was originally owned by a 'Mr. George' when my Auntie Bianca and Uncle Mondo purchased it in the early 1950's. It was appropriately named *Beach Road Coffee Shop* because of its location and with such a close proximity to Dofasco, it immediately earned the patronage of the employees. At the time, my Auntie Muffie was a much valued member of the staff filling the roles of both cook and baker of the soon-to-be infamous pies.

After a few years, an amicable buy out ensued and the restaurant was renamed *Muffie's Coffee Shop*. A newer and more coveted spot on Ottawa Street at MacNulty in northeast Hamilton was secured but still catered to the hardworking and ravenous steelworkers. Seven days a week they would start lining up as early as 6:00 am and continue well into the evening hours as they yearned for her open kitchen, freshly prepared and homemade Italian dishes and pastries. The only use for the patrons' metal lunch boxes was to cart away any leftovers to enjoy at their next break. And long lineups at the cash were never an issue as she merely ran tabs for each one of them, all good for the money at the end of each month. Every one of them had a story and Auntie Muffie's heart welcomed and absorbed each one.

The shop was pure amusement to my siblings and me. It was always our first stop on our weekly road trips from Thorold to Hamilton for my mother's family fix. You see my mom was the only one to move away so the frequent visits were mandatory for both her *soul* as it was her time to get caught up on all family news and her *soles* ... as she loved to look at the new selection of shoes in those high-end stores on Main Street.

Back to the shop. The seating was a combination of low swivel chrome stools surrounding the curved counter which overlooked the cooking area, a selection of arborite tables and vinyl covered chairs arranged in the middle, and three booths for more cozy and cloistered dining along the wall.

There was an unspoken rule that the end booth was reserved for family and staff. Back in that corner many a dispute was settled, personal news delivered and local shopping specials shared. The next booth was for us kids. And we knew that aside from opening our mouths to sip our ice cold Coca Cola bottle fresh out of the water-filled cooler and munch on our greasy fries doused in gravy, we must not make a sound ... in alignment with the nostalgic philosophy: *children should be seen and not heard.* So it was from that position of silence that I devoured everything that Muffie's Coffee Shop had on the menu ... literally.

My consumption though went well beyond the milkshakes from the aptly named Hamilton Beach appliance, the daily special pasta and meatballs, the side of peas and mushrooms and I can't forget those delicious homemade pies. Of course that all filled my ever expanding belly each week but it was the *goings on* around me I paid most attention to and enjoyed.

The sights, smells and sounds from Muffie's Coffee Shop remain deeply embedded in the base of my brain. Watching the activity each visit was as good as a weekly episode of any sitcom. The aroma was an interesting blend of sizzling Italian cooking in Unico, the best olive oil of the time, the sweat and grime of the stained coveralls and the low hanging smoke that filled the air from my aunt's *on the go* cigs, which gingerly balanced on the phone, the end of the table or lower corner of her mouth … often all at the same time.

The phone rang constantly and not just for take-out orders. Often it was my aunt's favourite clothing store telling her about a new shipment that just arrived in her size that she'd definitely want two of, or a hushed voice offering a tip on the next horse race (just in case one of the diners might be interested) and at times it was one of the suitors of the young women who worked there. Many a romance began within the walls of the shop and blossomed over that stainless counter.

Although the staff generally consisted of relatives and family friends there was one person who was neither. His name was Billy. He lived in the neighbourhood and his relationship with the restaurant began with daily visits. It was where he felt both at home and accepted. He was a big chunk of a simple man, and with a drooping lower lip that dripped saliva as he spoke in his uniquely high pitched yet mumbling manner. Although perhaps not physically appealing, his eyes did sparkle at the sight of my aunt.

Billy craved her attention and would do anything for her, knowing of course that she took exceptional care of him and catered to his wellbeing for both nourishment and petty cash. He was quickly welcomed into the family fold and given odd jobs as his contribution. He was particularly proud of his mopping skills and stacking ability of the pop bottle crates in the corner. However, he was most adept at staying away from the watchful eye of my Uncle Fred, whose primary role in the restaurant was to cast a critical eye over the 300 square feet space … hence the vow of silence I reluctantly adopted at each visit. Like us kids, Billy knew his place and he was happy there.

Many a family function was held there after closing hours as my Aunt willingly extended her work day. Although it was not a typical home to welcome guests, she was more than generous with her hospitality. By the time her own son Gene became employed by the local steel company, those on his shift also reaped the benefits of his schedule. If their time card required hours on a holiday, Auntie Muffie went out of her way to offer a special meal to the entire crew. What she could not do within her own crowded back shop living space, she more than made up for out on the linoleum floor of the restaurant.

The coffee shop was Auntie Muffie's life as she sacrificed all else. Although her closets were full of the latest fashions, she frequently lacked the energy to attend the functions that required them. Her family yearned for more time with her but settled instead for what she could provide for them. And ultimately the declining health of her husband was the siren alerting her to what she had been missing. She eventually sold the shop in 1976, retired, and enjoyed her first taste of normalcy.

It was during those years of her retirement when we all truly got to enjoy her character and generous spirit. Gone was the drawn face of fatigue, the incessant puffing of the smokes and the drone of the *24-7* life she had committed to for well over 25 years. With the restaurant world and worries behind her, a more fun, relaxed and joyful Auntie Muffie emerged as she embraced her new life eager to fill the voids her past life created. And we savoured every moment of that time until her death in 1989.

Muffie's Coffee Shop was a strong and vibrant thread both in the fabric of our extended family as well as the community surrounding it in the northeast end of Hamilton. And I know for certain if it were standing today the line ups would be as long, the diners as hungry and the calorie laden homemade dishes consumed with as much gusto.

Whether the coffee shop is listed in the city archives as one of the all-time great diners or not I'm sure that each of her patrons still treasure their own memory of it. As for me, I am most grateful to have her stools lining the bar in our basement and her milkshake maker on the counter. But ohhhh, what I would do for a slice of her pie.

A Titse Fly By

One year for my birthday, my friend Carol planned an outing for us to enjoy together. We met at a Conservation area mid way between her place in Drayton and mine in Oakville. The plan was to start our day with a long walk so we could get caught up followed by shopping and lunch.

Since we met so early, the parking lot was empty and there appeared to be no one else on the trail. Being late April, we were dressed in layers for comfort from the chilly spring air.

As we headed further along the trail I began to feel what appeared to be something minute biting at my skin beneath my bra. Although irritated, it did not keep my chin from wagging in continuous chatter with my friend. Every so often I would squeal and whack at my left breast in hopes to squelch whatever might be there.

At one point I even dropped my hand through the various layers and into my bra to determine if there was actually something there. Still nothing.

After about ten minutes of the steady barrage of nibbling, I decided I had had enough of the incessant irritation. I quickly looked around to make certain no one else was in sight. I then reached into and through my clothing layers yet again. Only this time I was dead set on not coming out empty handed.

In one fell swoop I reached in to cup my left breast and lift it right out into the cool air. The culprit was the teeniest bug. And at the precise moment I flicked it away, a male cyclist sped out from the path behind us to pass. Struggling to maintain his balance from the surprise spotting he whipped his head around and screamed, "Holy s**t ... you just made my day."

After that he could have broken out in song but neither Carol nor I could have heard him through our own squeals.

Our laughing continued as we traipsed along the trail.

Twenty minutes later when we had finally settled down and forgotten the incident, the cyclist reappeared on a neighbouring path.

When he spotted us he waved excitedly and yelled out, "Hey, thanks again eh? I'll never forget you."

The Quick Pitch

One cool November day I sat at a busy intersection waiting patiently for the light to turn green. When I looked across several lanes of traffic I spotted an older man standing on the median. He looked to be at least 75, and was carrying a gas container and car battery. He was bundled up, but I could see that under his coat, he was dressed in a shirt and tie.

It was obvious he had an issue with his car, wherever it was parked. I was intrigued and wondered how far he had already walked and how much further he had to go. It made me think of my own father, knowing how determined he would have been to solve any problem he faced. I felt sorry for this man because it was nippy out and I watched sympathetically as he approached the car beside me to ask for a lift. The driver motioned to the back seat where the baby seat was affixed, indicating that there was no room for him. He then spotted my car, proceeded to weave around the cars, and approached me with the same request. Acting before thinking, I nodded when he asked me if I was headed north and before I knew it, he was in my car.

He greeted me with, "Aren't you afraid of me?"

I wondered to myself, Buddy, aren't you afraid of me? Then it hit me. I guess I was taking a risk. Looking back at the people in the car that had first rejected him, I could see them staring at me with concerned looks on their faces. They seemed to be saying, "Are you sure you want to do this? Signal if you need help."

Too late to change my mind, I shrugged my shoulders and winced helplessly in their direction. Feeling apprehensive, I figured that I would soon find out whether I had just made a colossal mistake.

His next attempt at conversation was to ask, "I guess you're in real estate?"

Having no clue where that presumption had come from, I responded, "No, actually I'm not."

"Oh, so what do you do?"

Trying not to be too specific, I replied, "I'm self employed."

Taking this opportunity to take control over the conversation's direction I then asked, "What do you do?"

"Well, I purchase bankruptcies for liquidation!"

Not waiting long enough for me to ask him to elaborate (so much for control), he continued enthusiastically, "For example, a load of jewelry was heisted at the airport. I put a low bid in and got the whole lot. Like, take these here watches."

He quickly pulled up both sleeves, and using his arms as showcases, he proudly revealed an assortment of watches. (Great, a watch guy.)

"I get these watches for as low as two bucks and I throw in the two batteries to boot. Would you like any?"

"Nnnoo, not really."

Next, he reached into his chest pocket and pulled out some folded papers. I cringed, afraid that it might be porn or something equally as bad.

He asked, "Are you a Newfie?" and flashed a comic strip at my face. "Look at this. Cute isn't it? It's about the recent maritime snowstorms! Completely non-offensive."

Distracted by the thought that maybe there was a hidden camera somewhere, I was slow to respond. Undeterred by my inertia, he jumped right back in and took the lead (which, of course, I had lost long before), boldly resurrecting the topic of my line of work.

"So, what exactly do you do?"

I know I could have used this as an opportunity to fabricate a career for myself, but I played it straight and told him that I was a professional speaker.

"Oh, really! Now, I can probably use your services."

He reached back into his pocket, pulled out a flyer about another one of his products, and without skipping a beat, gushed, "Heck, as a matter of fact, I have a sample right here!" A return to his pocket and the sample was provided.

With all this going on, I'm surprised that I managed to stay within my own lane as I drove the two miles to his destination. As I thankfully pulled into the gas station, he asked for my phone number. He figured I could probably do some work on his behalf and speak for him.

Politely, I replied, "No, I'm sorry I couldn't do that." And then he was gone.

I wasn't attacked; I wasn't offended; and thank goodness, I didn't even have to reach for my wallet. But he sure didn't waste any time making his pitch! As I continued on my way, I couldn't help but watch him in my rearview mirror. I was confident he was headed back across the street to play out the scenario once again … with yet another unsuspecting customer.

Funeral Limo

*F*unerals are serious affairs. The more serious the affair the more difficult it often is to contain your emotions. Ever felt like laughing hysterically in church? We have all had to swallow an outburst at one time or another.

When my father-in-law Giorgio passed away, Joe and I were joined in the family limo by four relatives. Not one of us weighed less than 200 pounds. My excuse was that I still retained something close to the size of the Oakville harbour in my body from the birth of my first child just a mere six weeks earlier.

The limo sat at the curb in front of the church with doors open, awaiting our arrival. As we stepped into the vehicle, a crowd gathered as a sign of support, waiting until we pulled away. Sitting there in the limo, I noticed two friends looking in. Our eyes met. I couldn't help but notice the strain on their faces that signified stifled emotion. I thought they were un-characteristically upset, until I realized they were suppressing laughter. It was obvious that something hilarious had caught their eye.

As I studied them, I noticed the others around them had also been affected. They motioned with their eyes: "Look over there" so I immediately followed their orders. What I saw con-cerned me because I knew how inappropriate it would be for me to even smile at this point, let alone laugh. But it soon be-came clear that my self control was about to be tested.

Apparently there was so much weight in the car that the corner of the right door had been punctured into the pave-ment. This meant the limo driver was unable to close the door.

To remedy this embarrassing situation, the driver very discreetly motioned to the usher nearby for assistance. After exchanged whispers, the usher went to the back left side of the car. Their plan unfolded: he sat on the trunk, thus lifting the front door off the pavement, allowing it to close.

I elbowed Joe to make him aware of the predicament. Our teeth gripped our lips to suppress any outburst that might not sound like an allowable wail. Unable to contain ourselves, we finally had to lower our heads and hold our breath, since continuing to watch would only fuel this mirthful fire.

The onlookers, too, did their best to suppress their laughter. In silence, Joe and I continued to clench our bellies until we got back into our own car, when we finally got to let it go.

Thank goodness for tinted windows ... and the added incentive to lose that *baby fat*.

The Tablecloth

*F*or many years one of our family traditions during the Christmas holidays was to spend a week at Camp Tawingo in Huntsville. It was a holiday we were fortunate to enjoy with many of our friends. One night my friend Jane and I were sorting through the costume room when we both zoomed in on an item that had been tossed on the concrete floor. It appeared to be a discarded white damask tablecloth.

Okay, it was dirty and wrinkled and had been stepped on many times but we could tell that it had been beautiful in a former life and had the potential to be restored to its rightful grandeur.

Jane fondly recalled her mother having a tablecloth just like it, which graced their dining room table during special dinners. As she reminisced I stood there staring at the sorry looking fabric, envisioning it laundered and returned to its original sparkling white.

I quickly decided this was a challenge I wanted to take on. I knew I could somehow resurrect this treasure and announced that I would be more than willing to do it for Jane. As I bragged about my laundering abilities I knew that if for some reason they failed there was always my mother, the queen of *whiter than whites* to fall back on. Excited, Jane gushed that she would cook an elaborate meal for us if I could somehow restore this tablecloth to its former beauty.

As soon as I got home my mission began. After a brief consultation with my mother I spot-sprayed it with a commercial stain remover then washed it in hot water. Next, I applied some lemon juice and soaked it. This was followed by another hot water wash. I then had a second consultation with my mother and she suggested that I use just a little bit of bleach, being very careful not to overdo it.

I added the bleach to another hot wash and saw that good things were starting to happen. The orphaned tablecloth was beginning to sparkle! I decided that one more load with the bleach would make the transformation complete and earn me much praise as well as the promised dinner.

Jane's excitement about my tablecloth project was mounting and she called me frequently to ask how it was going. Encouraged by my reports, she said that she could actually picture it gracing her own antique dining room table.

I wanted so badly to make good on my promise to Jane. One more load, and that would be it. I'd dry, iron, fold and deliver it to her and my job would be done. I could almost taste that wonderful dinner!

With great anticipation I took the tablecloth out of the washing machine for the last time. I immediately sensed that something was amiss. What were those strings looped around the agitator? Why did the tablecloth suddenly look so small, wrapped around the walls of the drum? Even the colour looked off.

As I pulled the cloth from the machine, it was screamingly apparent that damage had been done and there was no way to fix it. I had messed up royally by adding just a little more bleach. The tablecloth was shredded, full of holes and I was initially devastated.

Not one to miss an opportunity for some fun, though, I told Jane next time she called, that I would deliver the tablecloth to her at the hairdresser's while she was getting her hair cut that afternoon. It would be an unveiling!

I gingerly ironed what was left of the poor tablecloth and made precise folds around the bit of cloth that was still intact. I then tied a ribbon around it for presentation. The little bundle looked ready to be placed lovingly on Jane's table.

When I arrived at the hair salon, Jane was still in the chair having her hair cut, but she urged me to unfold the tablecloth right away so she could savour its restored beauty. I carefully complied. When the final fold dropped, so did Jane's jaw. Still holding up the ruined tablecloth, I cringed as I waited for her reaction.

Luckily, the stylist was smart enough to put down her scissors when she realized there was no way she could safely continue while Jane convulsed with laughter.

Later it occurred to me that the lesson in this story is that sometimes things are good enough the way they are. Not everything needs to be changed, fixed or modified in our sometimes overly zealous quest for perfection.

I still got the dinner.

Viewer Discretion Advised

Although Joe and I are part of the Yuppie generation, we have strived to resist most of the practices that being a Yuppie entails. One example involved the use of the video camera with our children. A part of me always cringed whenever I attended a children's concert, game or ceremony and witnessed hordes of parents jockeying for the best position from which to film.

My usual approach to these circumstances was to sit quietly amidst the parental mayhem, maybe take a picture or two, putting whatever energy I had into enjoying the moment at hand. In fact, by the third child, I pretty much just told her to try her best to record her own life. I never lost enthusiasm for celebrating all of her accomplishments, but I had just about tilted in my efforts to document everything that happened in my children's lives.

However, we still did own a video camera. It left our home no more than half a dozen times. From the beginning, I had a different plan for its use. My idea was to bring it out once a year, on New Year's Eve, for a fireside chat with our family.

Our first filming took place on December 31, 1985. It had been a momentous year with both the death of Joe's dad, Giorgio, and the birth of our first child, Dante. The stage was set. Camera on tripod, battery charged, seats placed in front of the fireplace and off we went. Or, to be more accurate, off I went.

For some reason, Joe was shy about participating in a one-way conversation and instead chose to nod in agreement as he sipped his wine. (Trust me; this in no way reflects our day-to-day communication style.) Recognizing his reluctance to talk to the camera, I eased into a lengthy monologue about the past year, segueing into plans for the next. I sprinkled my presentation with intermittent questions to Joe, giving him the opportunity to share his own thoughts if the need arose (I always knew I could be a talk show host).

We continued in this way until the tape was completed. The more I talked, the more animated I became and the more animated I was, the more graphic were the details. Nothing escaped my attention; I described our pre-pregnancy activities, the conception, each trimester and ultimately the very long labour and delivery. I acted it all out, spewing forth every thought that had been carefully stored in my still youthful memory bank. Knowing that the video was for private viewing only, I did not hold back. Peppered with profanity, I expressed exactly how I felt about every intimate and gory detail. It was cleansing. I enjoyed flushing out my brain immensely. We popped the tape out, labeled it and tucked it away in the cabinet.

Time passed. Joe and I were heading out one evening after welcoming a new babysitter into our home. She seemed like a very nice responsible girl and had brought along a few of her favourite videos to watch while we were out. Hours later when we returned, she was quick to outline the full events of the evening with our baby. On her way out the door, she turned her head and added off-handedly, "Oh, and I REALLY enjoyed watching your video. That was so funny."

Did I detect a muffled snicker as she reached for the door behind her? I suddenly grasped the full implications of her comment as the highlights of the tape flashed through my head. In hindsight, I guess I should have reprimanded her for looking at our private stuff, but I was so paralyzed by embarrassment that I said nothing.

Whenever I saw that babysitter during the years that followed, I found myself wondering how much she had shared with her friends and family, and sheepishly danced around any conversation that might confirm my worst fears. From that night on, however, our private videos were stored with the cleaning supplies. They never looked there.

Tai Chi

In the late 1980's, different forms of relaxation and recreation were emerging to offset the newly acknowledged stresses in our lives. Admittedly, I was guilty of leading just that sort of life and although I had always exercised, I preferred to participate in what I call high octane activities like running, basketball, baseball, tennis and aerobics. I liked fast paced, powerful forms of movement and if music was involved, even better.

One fall, someone suggested I give Tai Chi a try. She raved about it and offered testimonials about the positive effect it had on her health and well-being. Apparently Tai Chi was a newly promoted yet ancient activity that was a moving blend of yoga and meditation. The words used to describe it in the Parks and Rec brochure were *soft, graceful and controlled*, none of which suited my nature or lifestyle. However, I had made a decision long before to try any form of recreation once. I signed up for the course.

Not having anything to wear besides neon Lycra aerobic wear which was *all the go* in the 1980's, I threw on a colourful collection of clothing for the first class. I ran the short distance from my home to the site. Once at the building, I bolted in and scanned the hallway for clues. I checked the notice board for the designated location and headed for the room.

As I entered the studio, I passed a handsome, statuesque, God-like creature standing to one side with his arms folded. I flashed a grin as I passed him and hurried into a room full of people in subdued clothing. I didn't make it far before hearing a deep voice softly rumbling up from behind me. "Stop. Please stop. Re-enter the room in peace."

Not knowing if he was talking to me, I glanced back. He didn't need to speak again because his eyes said it all: "I mean you."

I turned around and with hands on my hips protested, "But I didn't do anything."

"You didn't have to," he replied softly, all Swami-like.

So I did as requested. I slowed my walk right down and tip-toed past him, thinking the noise he had referred to was coming from my footsteps. Who knew that my energy and aura could be so loud? Knowing I was now a marked participant I found a spot in the back corner, where I figured I could stay out of trouble and hide if necessary.

Once the group was gathered, the deity took his place in front. In a low, sensual voice, he used words like peace, calm and tranquil in relation to the balance, energy and rhythm of our bodies. His tone and demeanor mesmerized me. Before I knew it, he was leading the class in flowing sets of movements that looked like dancing but which never seemed to end. Stumbling along from the back, not having a clue what to do I asked, "Uh, I'm new here; will you be teaching these moves to us?"

He shook his head.

"Are there any posters I can look at to learn them? I am a visual learner."

Without interrupting his movements, he again responded with a silent no. My last attempt: "Any music I can follow?"

"Absolutely not."

Then, mercifully responding to the pleading look on my face he said, "Just follow. It will come to you naturally."

Well, there I stood, squinting around to find the best person to follow. I settled on one accomplished senior and desperately tried to mimic her every move. It was futile. The series of movements was designed to take 17 minutes but I was done in 12 minutes. It created so much stress for me that I was a bundle of tension by the time I got home.

I gamely hung in for four of the six weeks, but it just wasn't worth the anxiety I experienced trying to grasp this new-ancient discipline and introduce my mind and body to a slower speed. Perhaps if I had given it more time and made a serious attempt to adopt it into my lifestyle, Tai Chi might have been the perfect antidote to my frenetic pace. I guess I was just too busy hurrying up to slow down.

Campus Centre Charade

When I went off to the University of Waterloo my world vastly expanded. Suddenly I was a part of a community of over 12,000 students compared to the intimate high school population of 500.

I was hungry to take in the sights of my new environment and I couldn't meet new people fast enough. Like a sponge, I absorbed whatever the campus had to offer. I guess you could say I majored in *People Watching* with a minor in *Socializing*.

My time away from academics was balanced between partying in the residence, surrounded by my new friends and seeking solace When I craved complete solitude to write in my journal, I'd retreat to my corner outside on the bench tucked behind the Humanities Building. There, amidst the shrubs and the trees, there was no view of the public, only the far away sounds of students hustling to class. A minimum of 15 minutes a day was spent in that hideaway.

My other favourite hangout was a popular spot called Campus Centre, familiarly known as the CC. I spent so much time there I claimed ownership to one of the public mailboxes located by the entrance. It was where I regularly retrieved notes from my friends.

People watching was an extreme sport in the CC. Low sinking chairs were arranged in a square along the perimeters of the main hall. Risk takers would stake their route from the main entrance to the other side of the building by bravely dissecting the square and walk directly through the open space into the other corner. The shy, inhibited types instead would choose the longer route along the outside of the square behind the chairs.

Between classes, I would frequently dash over there to get a ringside seat. It was nonstop entertainment and you never knew what sightings would be made each day.

The regulars included the *potheads* who would spend most of their day smoking up in one of the upstairs offices then retreat to sleep off leftovers sprawled over one of the chairs. A few whose home was the large computer in the sky (the Math building) could frequently be seen parading through the room with their hand positioned to form a G shouting "GAUS LIVES." The jocks in their black and yellow team jackets were known for cockily strutting directly through the middle of the square on route to the gym broadly swinging their arms or at least their rackets. They clearly wanted to be seen. And others would simply use the CC as their meeting spot to have a few laughs together or enjoy an ice cream cone as they waited for their next class. To a muse like myself, it was a mecca for material.

This also meant that I too was a familiar fixture. I even had my one particular chair which I claimed ownership to. But, interestingly I never worried about being part of anyone else's eye feast or being the source of entertainment. No. After all, I was the audience and they nourished me. I could barely keep up with my writing of the daily escapades of the CC in my journal.

Until one day when I was lounging comfortably well back into my chair. Though my body was relaxed and still, my eyes excitedly darted about desperately not wanting to miss a thing. I glanced over towards the main door and noticed a group of *Artsies* congregating. Typically they wore odd yet interesting combinations of clothing; skipped through campus arm in arm belting out Shakespearean sonnets; and were generally so uninhibited they remained oblivious to any onlookers because they had the courage not to care (an admirable trait). The entire campus was their stage.

As I sat there I studied them. One by one I watched them

gather, hug and slowly form a huddle. It appeared that something was about to take place and luckily for me, I had my ringside seat for maximum pleasure. I sat up, repositioned myself and anxiously waited for the performance.

The leader surfaced from the centre of the throng. Dressed entirely in black from bolero to boots it was evident he possessed the most dramatic flare of the group. He proceeded to lead the others into the middle of the CC with one arm searching through the air like a tai chi expert. Someone grabbed his other waving arm and they linked hands, each moving in unison. Another joined them. This continued until the entire group of seven was connected.

They paraded through the centre open area with arms flailing through the air in slow motion. And as they slithered about they chanted a slow deliberate chorus of, "We're step-ping through mol-las-ses and we want you to come a-long."

Over and over they recited these words. As they slow-ly and deliberately moved around the room, the person at the end scanned the room for any eager bystanders. As each was chosen, they reached out for their hand and gently yanked them into the group to join in. The line quickly extended to over twelve.

My heart raced as I watched. I sank lower into my front row seat as I tried to minimize my aura and pray I would not be noticed. My head retreated deeper into its shell. Nervously I swallowed a lump and hoped I could suddenly melt into the stained fabric of the chair. As I sat waiting for the impromptu parade to end, I found myself smiling. Not an 'oh I feel so good, this is so delightful' smile but a definite 'oh please, whatever you do, don't you dare pick me' nervous kind of smile. My eyes opened wider as they headed my way. Where is the escape hatch in these seats when you need it?

Suddenly the row of seating behind me had its own benefits. Before I could scream, "NOOOOO!" loud enough to startle any potheads from their dead sleep, I was whisked up by a person who seemed entranced by the whole experience.

Slowly we moved, sweaty palms together, arms weaving through the imaginary molasses chanting as one. My head lowered as my eyes rolled back into my forehead. With my racing pulse I managed to fake joining them in their chant. Instead I mumbled my own version: "Will-some-one-pul-lease-help-to-get-me out-of-here?" All the while I cringed and prayed none of my friends were there to enjoy this scene.

When it was over I darted to my chair to retrieve my belongings. With head down and heart pounding I dashed out of the CC shaken to my core. It took me two weeks before I got the courage to return to my post.

P.S. I am proud to say I've come a long way in the courage department since that episode. Inhibitions? Nah. Thankfully, on that day, they left the building.

One Chair, No Waiting

I must admit that since I have become a gardener, I look at hair differently. I pay more attention to it and readily notice the flaws. With shears always within reach, I am capable of a good pruning job at any time. My nonpaying customers are generally males in need of a buzz cut. Upon noticing some excess fuzz, I can have the electric clipper plugged in before they know I have the cape draped around them. The real fun is leading them to believe I've done a great job, then purposely leave one tuft, out of their line of vision.

Well I'm not ready to register my business One Chair No Waiting, but I am improving. I seem to get most satisfaction attacking my own hair, usually when I'm bored. It innocently starts with a minor tweak around the ears. The next day, I indulge in a blind snip of the back. And it slowly progresses into a full frontal lean over the wastebasket with shears snapping into the top layer of my head.

I blindly hack and chop and thanks to *product* I can generally make it work. If it doesn't, hats and turtlenecks do wonders to cover up the slips. But I will admit that I sometimes feel I am only one bad hair day away from looking like Captain Kangaroo. Thankfully I am confident that the *make-up cut* with Cecil is just a phone call away.

Just last week I was standing at a street corner waiting to meet my friend Deb for coffee. A woman walked past and crossed the street. I watched her stop, turn around and head back towards me. She walked right up to me and said, "Who cuts your hair?" I was surprised by her question.

"You came back across the street to ask me that?"

"Yes it caught my eye. I like the look. Where do you go?"

"Well actually I've been cutting it myself for the past few months (boredom)."

We chatted, shared hair horrors and styling secrets. After a few minutes she left and I joined my friend.

Later as Deb and I walked through the nearby parking lot, the woman suddenly pulled up beside us in her car. "Oh I'm glad I saw you again. I forgot to get your number. I'd love for you to cut my hair. I'll call you."

She caught me off guard and I stupidly gave her my number.

Now if she does call, I'm going to have to confess that I'm really a fraud and that I couldn't possibly accept responsibility for her head of hair. Or perhaps I can say that the chair's being occupied (by three layers of coats) unless of course she'd be happy with a *buzz*. If not, I do have extra hats.

Still Proud of My Badge

I was once a Brownie. Once a Brownie, always one. I remain a friend of the Girl Guides of Canada (as they hold treasured spots in my mind as many of my favourite audiences). And to this day I hold the 1960's motto *Lend A Hand* close to my heart ... so much so it is part of my new tattoo.

For me being a Brownie extended far beyond being able to meet with friends after school hours. It wasn't even wearing that sandy brown outfit (the colour of poop) that never quite fit my overlarge body with tights too short and hem too high. And it didn't help that we then had to wear a belt to accentuate the waist I was not blessed with, thus tugging the outfit even higher up my chubby torso. But I did love that change purse that rested comfortably on the left side of the belt, storing the weekly dues ... especially the way it snapped closed. Simple mind, simple pleasure.

The highlight was not even the tie that I struggled to learn to knot or even the dancing pixie promise pin that remained centrally affixed in a prominent position. I loved the games, the fun and being with my friends. Heck I still remember the ditty we sang: *"We are the sprites … brave and strong like the knights."* (Oh the useless things I can remember.)

No, all that aside, what I really loved was earning the badges. You see I have the collector gene. I worked towards collecting those Brownie badges with the same intensity that now drives me to amass junk for my garden (I've run out of indoor space ... and NO I am NOT a hoarder). And it helped that my mom was a seamstress so they were always instantly and beautifully attached to the uniform, unlike my own daughter's. If there weren't any staples handy I used butterfly clips or the glue gun. She was sweet enough to never complain.

Looking back, although I can recall many badges that I would still qualify for, there is one that stands out ... *The Good Neighbour.* Yes, I do love to offer a helping hand or whatever else might be needed. If you're seeking assistance, advice, opinions, I'm at your service.

Proudly I can boast I am still most deserving of that *Helpful 'n Hospitable* badge.

Sometimes I think I'm so smart, like people actually want to hear what I have to say. I actually look for opportunities to interject, offer my opinion or at least my aid to some needy person nearby. I see myself like that person in the Esso Gasoline commercial in the 1960's who pledged, "Esso Information. Ask me anything. I'm here to assist you."

I often give directions: "C'mon, you can follow me. I'll get you there ... and if not, we can at least enjoy a coffee together." Or I'll comment on how the outfit they're trying on really looks: "Ah, I wouldn't listen to that salesperson ... the other colour is more your palette and will bring out the colour of your eyes." Or frequently I go on *purse patrol* stopping shoppers (usually at Costco). "Excuse me, you really shouldn't leave your purse in the buggy. It can easily get stolen."

But I have learned that such unsolicited *two cents* aren't always welcomed as a shopper once looked at me after the purse comment and said, "Well if it means that much to you!" as she yanked her purse from the buggy and tucked it under her arm. I muttered, "Geez I was just trying to help … you deserve to have it stolen" and sheepishly moved on, secretly hoping my error in judgement still qualified me for the badge.

However sometimes my willingness to comment does work. When Parker's Cleaners first opened in our local mall, I immediately noticed that the colouring of the newly erected sign was all wrong. Although absolutely none of my business, I was still concerned. A few days later when I was in the grocery store (to buy licorice - I do not buy groceries … that's Joe's department) I happened to see the guy from Parker's. I had never met him but he looked like he might be easy to approach. I tapped him on the shoulder, introduced myself and shared my concern with him about the visibility (or lack) of his new business.

He listened and appeared half intrigued … not by my signage savvy but more by my gall to impose my suggestion that he had just wasted his money. Coincidently, a few weeks later, I noticed the sign was replaced with one that was more visible and easily read.

Twenty years have passed and Dave, from the cleaners still shows his gratitude by treating me as a valued customer. I was in there the other day and noticed he has hired a seamstress. Hmm, I think I'm going to have her reinforce that badge for me.

P.S. I know this story made you dizzy to follow … heh sometimes that's just how the mind works … notice I never bragged about the *Focus* badge.

You Can't Make Me ...

*E*arly in our relationship (circa 1976), Joe and I were driving in downtown Hamilton on a windy, summer night. Relying on his intuition and concerned I was somewhat chilled (could it have been my staring out the passenger window with my arms crossed that triggered the thought?).

Blessed with the caring gene, Joe said, "You cold? You can have my jacket." It was a red nylon school team jacket.

"No, it's okay. I'm fine (a female's favourite saying)."

"Here, I'll take it off. I don't need it."

"Joe, I'm fine, I don't need your jacket."

He started wiggling out of his jacket as he drove and persisted in his attempt at chivalry.

"C'mon it'll warm you up."

"Joe, I don't need your flippin' jacket."

Determined to change my mind, he continued, "Here, c'mon just put it on."

That was it. My *tipping point* had been reached. My stubborn needle was at *max* and there was no way he was going to make me change my mind. I grabbed the jacket from my side, rolled down the window and released it into the open air.

As the expletives filled the interior, I watched the jacket dance into the night breeze through the rearview mirror. By the time he circled back to retrieve it, it was gone ... hopefully providing warmth for someone who really needed and wanted it.

We never spoke of it again.

Many, many years later after our family misplaced yet another item, I commented that I couldn't wait to get my hands on the phantom retriever of all of our belongings that had somehow gone astray. I pictured him wearing Dante's new Nikes, Joe's good watch, Vince's treasured ball cap, riding Alena's birthday bike and carrying my beloved baseball glove.

Joe was quick to pipe in, "And wearing my red jacket."

Seasoned Junkers

The annual scheduling of Junk Week in Oakville lasted about ten years. It was a time each spring when we could discard items that were no longer used, wanted or worked. It was a cultural event for many.

Each year, prowlers got gutsier and gutsier in their shopping. The seasoned shoppers typically drove a pickup and were armed with a large supply of bungee cords. Often travelling at night, it was not uncommon to look out and see them searching through the heap wearing a miner's lamp. They'd sort through your trash with an eye for the *specials*, i.e. anything with metal content that could be sold for scrap.

The rest of us just made sure to allow plenty of time whenever we drove anywhere, to allow for emergency pull-overs and slowly paced drive-bys. I hated getting scooped by anyone who carted away a great find that I myself had been eyeing.

I was always on the hunt for anything unique that could live happily in my garden, since Joe had long ago forbidden me to bring anything else through our front door. These pirated treasures never failed to make for an interesting garden tour.

In recent years I buddied up with my friend Carol Ann, who is herself a seasoned scavenger. We figured that by travelling together we could always have a lookout person. We could often be found dashing from one heap to another while the car sat idling in the middle of the street with both doors open. More than once we had to race back when aggravated drivers honked for us to move. It was just so easy to get lost in the hunt.

During our travels we have been invited into people's

homes, combed yards for that one missing part and been frequently stared at from behind drawn curtains as we carefully critiqued each item.

Carol Ann and I are good at sharing our finds, but we are not above battling over the occasional item that we both claim to have seen first. We will also drag, hoist or jam a precious gem into the van even though we have no plan for it. Some trash is just too darn good to pass up.

But unlike a lot of scavengers, we will not succumb to selling the goods. We're proud of our pieces and display them like hunters would show off their souvenir pelts.

For a few years we booked off Junk Week as vacation time, even though we were not employed anywhere. It was a great way to learn the streets of Oakville. Many times you could hear one of us say, "Oh, I know that street. That's where we got the dining room table and eight chairs."

After several years Halton Region went to a different model for junk collection. Instead of assigning one week for all of Oakville, different areas were designated, each with their own Junk Week. My goodness, we were ecstatic: eight different weeks to go *trashing*!

That summer Carol Ann and I really got to know each other because we approached our junking like a part-time job. We were so happy with the weekly adventures that I sent the Region an email expressing my appreciation for the opportunity to extend my street shopping days. We were particularly pleased with the return policy: if for some reason we were not satisfied or happy with our choice we could just drive it to another location and dump it. No hassles, no questions, no forms to fill out, no line ups. For all of this we were very grateful.

Just as we were getting used to the new system they changed it again and unfortunately it wasn't nearly as much fun. For starters, it is no longer referred to as Junk Week. It is now called Bulk Collection. I guess a tony town like Oakville really doesn't have junk - just bulk.

To carry on with our quest to find the best bulk now requires a continuing education course. We must first determine the location of the eight distinct regions, then study the collection calendar to learn which days have been designated for pickup in each of them. To make things even less fun, there is a three-item limit with all kinds of restrictions. Gone are the days of mounds as high as snow banks filled with everything from the likes of fridges, tires, and picnic tables. And they are not to be put out until the night before the trucks come to pick them up. So how do they ever expect us to get there in time?

Nevertheless, we are trying to make the best of it within the confines of the new system. Our hunger for the hunt is as intense, but we both agree it's just not the same. Now most of our fun comes from reminiscing about the *good old days* ... "Remember the day we had to leave you behind because you couldn't fit? Remember the day we had to push the guy off his bike for fear he would get to that lamp before us? Remember how we furnished the boys' condo when they went off to university?" It was amazing.

So now as we wait for next season to hit the streets again, we're happy to sit back and revel in the oohs and ahs of our friends when they look around our yards and ask, "Where'dja get that?"

Proudly we reply in unison, "The Junk."

I think we're ready to take on the scrap metal.

Thanks for Helping, Joe

When Joe and I lived in the apartment, pre-kids, we enjoyed having people over to celebrate just about anything ... Grey Cup, first snowfall, end of school, any opportunity to get together. We still do this, except now it's often a month-long challenge trying to come up with a date that is convenient for everyone.

I remember one night when we had four couples over for dinner. We had had lots of laughs, and it was after midnight when they finally left. Joe and I were both exhausted, but since he had cooked the meal, I was on clean-up duty. Before he went to bed, however, he was good enough to ask if he could help me out. (I was glad that he hadn't missed the whiny tone in my voice when I innocently inquired, "You're not going to bed already, are you?") Shamelessly I accepted his offer.

"Sure Joe, just shake the tablecloth over the balcony to get rid of all the crumbs. And be careful, it's windy out there."

Joe considerately did what I asked while I whipped through the kitchen doing what I do best: creating order. I had the kitchen sparkling in record time before heading off to bed.

The next day my mission was to attack the rest of the previous night's mess, which meant doing the laundry. I had pitched the tablecloth into the hamper, but I couldn't seem to find the matching napkins. I shook Joe to wake him up. "Joe, where are all the napkins?"

He growled, "How the heck should I know?" and rolled over to continue his snooze.

I was mystified by their disappearance. I sifted through the garbage that was already tied and ready to be dropped down the chute. No napkins. I checked under the table. I called my dinner guests to see if maybe they had snuck them away as a souvenir of the night. No napkins. By the time Joe finally got up, I had worked myself into a frenzy. Remembering that he had been the one on tablecloth duty I immediately snapped at him: "What did you do with all those napkins? They were left on the table. You tell me how ten napkins can disappear over-night!" (Subtle I was not.)

He was adamant. "There were no napkins."

As the hangover from the night before started to clear, I got a flash of recall. I reminded Joe, "They must have been on the tablecloth when you shook it out over the balcony."

Together we ran outside and peered over the railing to the 10 floors below. Sure enough, there they were. Two were stuck in trees. One had landed on the roof of the indoor pool. Three appeared to be on balconies on the third floor. Two lay daintily on the roof of a car in the parking lot, as if waiting for a phantom waiter to come and complete the place settings. The final two were waving from the railings of apartments immediately below us.

We spent much of that afternoon retrieving the wayward napkins, and managed to make an excellent impression when we had to knock on the doors of strangers and greet them with, "Hi, we're your new neighbours. Can you do us a favour and pass the napkins?"

Thoughts 'n Things About Thongs

The following is a daily account of my 14-day trial of wearing a thong, August 22 - September 4, 2010. Please read at your own risk as you might find some of the visuals disturbing.

I fondly remember some of my best underwear from my childhood going back as far as the full-briefed cotton with ruffled edges and little flowers to the seven pack days of the week. All were worn as high up the torso as allowed. Early adulthood got me set on Jockey french cut, sitting not too high and not too low with leg bands that weren't tight enough to dig in or loose enough to ride up.

Most recently I expanded into a more diverse selection ... some with panels to pull fat away (to where?), some of miracle fabric to blend into the skin of the butt and some blessed with extra Lycra for improved stretch. But the drawer is now heavy on the favourite Jockey silk line which allow my clothes to move freely with every stride.

I have been happy with my daily choices which varied depending on my activities of the day. I never once yearned for something smaller, even sexier. Besides, like beauty, I believe it's underneath that counts. I used to squirm seeing young women bend over exposing the thread like 'T' fabric of their thong above their hipsters. Finding it comical, I once vowed I would get a tattoo of the same scene on my backside so when I died the undertaker would get the last laugh as he flipped me over.

Then the day I turned 50, my dear friend Babbi gave me a gift-wrapped, sleek black, angular piece of cloth with instructions: "Wear it all day."

OMG what the hell is it? Where exactly do I wear it? Is it a form of head gear? A facemask?

Surely it does not belong below the waist to protect the coveted triangle, the area engineered with a protective covering designed to attract the opposite species. So does the narrow part of this *thing* sit at the front so as not to cover the eye candy? I don't think so. That would surely create a distinct division much like yanking your mouth toward your ears. Now I know some just might find pleasure in this but the thought of it made me wince. OK, then the narrow panel must go the back ... but wait there is nearly not enough fabric to go anywhere other than down and through the slitted area into the abyss.

Once I had it on and was assured it was in the correct location, I shrieked as I struggled to catch a glimpse of what I had created. Darting around like a dog chasing his tail I tried to steal scenes from the various angles and was not happy. And I was definitely not looking forward to my day spent wearing it.

Without going into too many details, the one scene I do remember quite vividly was taking part in a NIA class of graceful movement and dance. At one point after trying to follow the rhythmic actions of our leader I froze in my tracks leaning to the right with outstretched arms to the future and back leg upward to the past. It must have been the look on my face that attracted the concern of our leader who immediately reacted with, "Are you OK?" I sheepishly responded, "I'm not sure. I think I just lost my thong."

The only other up close encounter was inadvertently washing one left behind in my son's dirty clothes hamper??

Fast forward eight years. I currently enjoy my drawer full of underwear, each with a specialty, beige for my white pants, low riders for my lower waisted pants, stretch cotton for gardening, sleek silk for dress pants, tummy tucker for those ill-fitted outfits and vividly colored for the dull days.

I have heard the younger women rave about the joys of the thong as I silently whisper, "Yeah right, I'd rather wear cardboard thank you." I have heard the recurring mantra, "Once you wear it you'll never go back" and "I'd never wear anything but."

Hence my crazy idea this summer to boldly announce (surely it was out of boredom): "OK fine, I'll try it for one week." But my friend Linda was quick to snap, "Nah. You have to try it for at least three weeks." I know it takes 21 days to break or make a new habit but I opted for the revised quick start edition and settled on 14 days of *trial separation*. KSB joined me in the challenge. Dian, once learning of the adventure was quick to throw her granny briefs into the ring as well.

The shopping trip to La Senza was a fun start as we yanked on various styles over our clothes in the open shop leaving the sales clerks shaking their heads at the foolishness. However once they learned of our challenge, they were quick to offer their input. They searched for the best suited, sized and styles for each of us, even allowing us to split the sale offering of five for $25 (I have since discovered I could have made the same trial purchase @ the Dollar Store for considerably le$$).

Once home, I studied the weather for the upcoming week. I was pleased to see that rain was forecasted. Maybe I could just stay in my pjs to avoid it a while longer.

In preparation, I took them out of the tissue and stared at them from all angles picturing, sensing and anticipating the experience I was so reluctant to have.

P.S. One note of optimism … I'm very thankful I no longer get my period because those micro-mini pads make me very, very nervous. Here goes …

Day 1: Thongs, in my mind were footwear that caused a rubber wedgie between my toes and that used to go flip flip as we walked. I can't even wear *them* anymore. What made me agree to this challenge?

Putting on the thong today reminded me of the elastic waist straps we wore to hold up our sanitary pads. Nervously I tugged it into position … the question being what is the proper position? I sensed right away it would be like trying to get used to wearing a mouth-guard to bed (which I have been doing for years now and am still not comfortable).

TTT (today's thong tip): Purposely wear a brightly colored top with baggy black bottoms to divert eyes away from the squirming and tugging.

Day 2: I chose a beige one with two micro mini waist bands which do nothing for holding in the inner tube which comfortably rests on my hips. The lack of support only means my buttocks look like two elephant ears flapping in the wind. So it's back to baggy bottoms.

TTT: Sit on your butt most of the day.

Day 3: I went looking in dread for the white one to wear today ... but it's so minute it had slipped into a corner of the drawer where it hid curled up like a scared bunny. I held off putting it on and instead, did the garden commando. Once showered and dressed with that first layer, I caught a glimpse in the mirror ... ouch. I don't care what degree of desperation an onlooker possesses, that cannot be an appealing sight of my rear.

Day 4: I went to The Bay and found myself longingly looking at other styles of undergarments. Never before have I given the selections such attention ... the truth being, my mother adds to my collection every Christmas.

Someone suggested to wear a thong in the next size up. Well, based on the limited selection of XL's available, there are an awful lot of smaller women sneaking into my size zone. So do they even make thongs for Plus Size?

Perhaps the more appropriate question is should they make thongs for Plus Size? Yes, I realize as a full-figured women I should be proud of my bounty of bootie ... but like anything else it doesn't mean I have to brag.

I finally made the reveal to Joe and as predicted he enjoyed a laugh out loud lasting a few moments. When he asked, "How does it feel?" (although I'm sure he was waiting for me to expound on the eroticism of its positioning) I only responded, "Like wearing that Band-Aid on the inside of your arm after a blood test and desperately waiting to rip it off."

Day 5: Golfing was not something I looked forward to … and I was right. From the first tee I felt I had a rubber patch on my butt hole. The sensation reminded me of when I was a little girl forced to wear hand me down bottoms from my older sister … and because I was bigger than her, the clothes were always too small for me. One bathing suit in particular took a ride up my butt as soon as I slipped into it … two steps forward, stop, yank, two steps forward … it really interfered with my fun. I can still hear the taunts: "Heh you got bugs?" and the familiar, "You goin' to the show? Pickin' your seat?"

TTT: I know fully understand that Irish saying: "Don't get your knickers in a twist."… It only makes you miserable.

Day 6: KSB came over with a new one for me to try. Excited about now having a six pair rotation, I put it on, on top of my capris. Joe didn't even notice. Finally when he did, he asked, "Does that actually cover everything?" The tongue in cheek response is, "Oh yeah there's more than enough fabric, you should try it." As CAS said, "And from the front it looks just like Binky the clown's wig." And no, there will not be a *brazilian* appointment booked any time soon.

Tonight I wore my new one to the funeral home. Suddenly I felt the right front side of my anatomy pop free. OMG a one-sided camel toe emerged right there at the visitation. I immediately said three Hail Mary's because clearly that was a sacrilegious moment.

TTT: Discovering the purpose of the thong is futile.

Day 7: Today, there was a whole lot of stickin' and pickin' goin' on. I wore the nice black and white leopard print with a thick lace band I had been saving. It certainly looked as though it might be comfortable. But unfortunately it lacked sufficient elastic to refrain from sliding below the belly roll giving a new twist to the term *drop and roll*. Regrettably they will be taken out of next week's rotation.

TTT: Don't wear a thong with rayon jersey pants.

Day 8: The shrinkage from the dryer does not help my cause so I'm now down to an assortment of three. I can't remember ever putting on underwear with this much prepping for proper positioning nor do I accept the proclamation: "You won't ever think about your underwear during the day." Hmmm I really don't believe I ever give my own familiar briefs any of my time except when I have been caught wearing my black ones with my light bottoms.

TTT: Be careful when tossing your thongs (that's if you can actually find them in the pile) into the washing machine. You end up getting 'ringers' around the 'whatever it's called'.

Day 9: I have to admit that other than the post 'pull up period' I rarely thought about it all day. But keep in mind it generally takes about 45 minutes for it to settle each time you have to pull it back up. And at my age with more frequent lavatory visitations the minutes of discomfort do add up.

So what was it today that diverted my attention from my own discomfort?

Was it the never-ending chatter between my mom and sister? Or perhaps it was the sitting for eight hours that kept things where they belong hence preventing me from any yanking?

TTT: Be still as long as possible

Day 10: I started the day knowing that KSB has already admitted she might be a new fan to the thong. I have never been a joiner or easily swayed so I will refrain from sharing my opinion until the end of Day 14, when at that time I will answer KSB's question: "Will it be an option or obsolete?"

Day 11: Today I wore white linen pants. My insecurities whispered that those *were* voices I heard from behind me as I scoured the aisles of Dollarama. I'm almost certain I heard cries of, "Not sure if she has underwear on or not ... wait, is that the outline of a thong I see framing that butt? OMG and at her age . Some women dress like they don't own a mirror."

Day 12: Yes things are settling somewhat. But in the same way as someone getting used to wearing a cast on their arm. Just because they've grown accustomed to it, doesn't mean they aren't looking forward to its removal.

Day 13: OK it's time to dig deep into my wardrobe and wear something tight around my butt. As conspicuous as it feels, I'm trying to convince myself that no one's looking there anyway ... not when I have such beautiful shoulders to stare at.

TTT: When wearing tight bottoms ... wear a very long shirt.

Day 14: I'm very excited that the trial is nearing the end. I purposely saved the best for last. Segue ... I remember once hearing a story about someone visiting the *cross store* ... a place to buy, sell or trade the *heavy cross* we carry through life. A woman went in, to trade her load because she felt it was too much of a burden. Ironically as she shopped around the store she soon discovered that one was too long, another too short, one caused splinters, one appeared to be off balance and the weight of the last one really hurt her back. However by the end of the search there was one cross that seemed to be perfect. Surprisingly it was the one she had brought in to trade.

So my best thong as it turns out is the one I received eight years ago for my 50th birthday. The one I frequently used as a prop to mock. The one I left unattended as the painful reminder of that day when I thought I had lost it somewhere deep within my crevices. Yes it ends up being the only one that is the least bit comfortable ... not considerably more but let's say I have the least discomfort wearing it. I will finish off the experiment with it.

I have now spent close to an hour searching for my treasured newly designated favourite thong ... the original black Jockey one. It is nowhere to be found. Could it be stashed within someone else's clean heap of clothes, caught in the corner of the sheets or has it gone to land of the unknown where dozens of our household single socks reside? I'm not happy.

TTT: Tag thongs with a brightly coloured ribbon when laundering.

The morning after ... ah I made it ... I can successfully tick it off the list with the note: *Bought them, wore them and lived to abhor them.*

God Bless you sworn convertors of all ages, shapes and sizes. Go nuts. I'm happy you're happy. But can we at least agree that *one woman's pleasure is another woman's pain?*

I'm now excited to resort to my drawer of briefs in all colours and styles and even add the Jockey's to my Christmas list again. I will however sift through them with more discernment eliminating any excess baggage.

I am proud to shout, "Bring on the panty lines ... I'm a big girl I can handle them." You shouldn't be looking there anyway. Why not check out the jewellery around my neck instead?

Also, I am seriously reconsidering my original tattoo design as the eternal reminder of the whole experience.

P.S. For Sale: 6 slightly worn thongs in size XL

    ... no reasonable offer refused

    ... 14 day documentation manual included

Written with pleasure August 22nd - September 5th, 2010

King Kong Bundy

*M*y size has always weighed heavily on my mind. So you can imagine the concern I faced when I discovered I was pregnant. After the usual expression of sheer delight (which is the politically correct response I'm sure), I couldn't help but fast forward to the potential weight gain I might endure. In discussion with Joe we decided on a goal to help keep me focused on a healthy pregnancy. Together, we calculated that at the time of delivery, my goal would be to not weigh more than Joe's (then) current weight of 207 pounds. Well, this certainly gave me plenty of room for my personal expansion project since my starting weight was a svelte 157.

Each month I was anxious about my appointment … not the intimate exploration by my physician, but the dreaded weigh-in by his nurse. I would schedule my appointment at the earliest time possible, purposely avoid breakfast, slip into an outfit of feather-weight texture and immediately remove any chunky jewelry. At the harsh command of the nurse I would daintily tip toe onto the scale (as though I was actually going to fool anyone) and hold my breath to avoid any heavy breathing.

Each monthly weigh-in recorded a substantial gain. Although I had maintained a rigorous fitness program throughout, I clearly could not escape the calories seeking comfort in my body. By the seventh month when I had still managed to avoid any pleasantries or eye contact with the nurse, it was time to once again step onto the scales. I held my breath as she slid the metal plate into position (she tried desperately for perfect balance) … 197 … 198 … 199 … 200 … 201. I gasped in horror at what I had seen and before I could exhale the nurse stepped back and let out a roar that surely woke the sleepy receptionist and any other weary patients in the waiting room. And as she roared she blurted, "I can't believe it, but you weigh over two hundred pounds!"

Embarrassed and hurt, I replied, "I don't think that's funny."

Two days later I sat in a weighting ... oops I mean waiting room at an X-ray clinic. With nothing to do other than sit and worry about the impending procedure, I decided to scan the current issue of *Time* magazine. Feature story June 1985 was an in-depth look at the world of *Wrestlemania*. I read with little to no interest until one of the photos caught my eye.

There in the bottom right corner was a picture of a person whose hair was cropped within an inch of his head and dyed white. My own hair at the time stood straight up as it, too, was closely cropped and the colour of salt and pepper. He was wearing what looked exactly like my one-piece black Lycra bathing suit (which I had worn in varying ways for the past seven years ... you know, straps down, one strap off the shoulder, sash around the waist ... anything to keep the style current). His body appeared to be shaped in the same barrel-like design as mine and was propped up with the support of similarly sized 'thunder thighs' and well-developed calf muscles. These similarities were grotesquely fascinating and I was intrigued enough to read on.

His name was King Kong Bundy. I read with great interest about how this person loved his job, enjoyed throngs of fans and in the process earned millions of dollars. And while our resemblance to one another did not exactly fill me with joy, it did make me smile.

That night, as I sat chatting with Joe I announced: "Joe, you won't believe this, but today I was reading a magazine and I saw a picture of a person who looks just like me ... same hair, same body and even the same bathing suit. His name is King Kong Bundy and he's a professional wrestler." By now, I'm actually laughing out loud about it.

Joe looked at me with both hurt and disgust in his eyes. "Aw, c'mon Carole, I don't like to hear you put yourself down like that. You're doing really well, you still look great and besides as long as you're healthy, who cares what you weigh?"

Joe just didn't get it. This was my way of coming to terms with my reality, and I managed to get a kick out of it.

A few nights later, as we visited with friends there was a lull in the conversation. Joe chose to speak. Smugly, he started, "So, what do you think of Carole? Don't you think she's looking a lot like King Kong Bundy?"

Everybody laughed. It was the entertaining line of the evening and they all marveled at what a funny guy he was.

All I could think of was, how dare he attack my self-image, his sensitive pregnant wife and use me as the butt of the joke in front of all these people?

Interestingly enough, this time I didn't laugh. And I wondered why all of a sudden Joe found it so funny.

Six weeks later, I entered the blissful state of labour, weighing in at 210. I had exceeded the goal we had set and Joe was now the lightweight. I held on to the extra weight well after the birth. The only thing that saved me was when I looked in the mirror I had to chuckle in spite of myself. Because you know, I really did look just like the KING!

I still think Joe needs to come up with his own material.

Your Honesty's Killing Me

Typically when I am about to start a presentation I feel like an athlete ready to take the field, so I was psyched to give this group everything I had for the next forty-five minutes. I stood in front of the 200 people who eagerly waited for me to live up to the introduction that they had just heard. I was ready and anxious to begin.

About five minutes into my talk, I noticed a woman seated in the front row to my right. She appeared to be in some discomfort. Distracted by this I stopped, leaned towards her and asked, "Are you okay?"

Holding her head in her hands, and looking at me woefully, she sighed, "Oh I'm fine. I just wasn't expecting it to be this loud. Will you be done soon?"

Of course I was taken aback by her question, but managed to reply, "Um, I just got started."

"Oh, heavens, I can't take this noise level or listening to you."

The only response I could manage was, "I think you just hurt my feelings."

Recognizing that I should not turn this into a spectacle, I backed away and promised I would stand as far away as possible from her and do my best to lower the volume with the hand-held mic.

I gamely continued speaking, although it was a challenge to ignore her discomfort with the presentation and distaste for me. At the mid-point of the talk I paused for some water and facetiously announced that if anyone felt like sneaking out, this would be a good time because I would be looking away. The woman took me up on the suggestion. Picking up her stuff she proceeded to march in front of the audience and head towards the back of the room. All eyes were on her, including my own. With all the restraint I could muster I refrained from making a comment.

At the conclusion of the presentation (which fortunately appeared to be a success) many people came forward to thank me. Some made comments about the woman but I chose not to respond. As I was packing up, the woman returned to the room, approached me and said, "I apologize for my behaviour earlier, but I really don't like motivational speakers. I have just heard so many."

Not feeling that I needed to convince her that I was not like all the rest, I sweetly replied through gritted teeth, "Oh that's okay, you are entitled to think that" ... and walked off.

A part of me wanted to stop, turn around and yell, "Oh, yeah? Well I'm not always crazy about some people in my audience either. So there!"

But thankfully I didn't. I held my head up and proudly strolled out of the auditorium. I had been humbled, but I wasn't going to let her get to me. As I made my exit I chuckled to myself. Little did she know but she had just given me a great opening for my next talk.

My Relationship with Sunshine

I don't know how my love of the *bennies* (beneficial rays of the sun) all started but I do rely on it as a mood booster. Is it the warmth it casts, the light it shines on our outdoor room or the way it colours our paled winter skin?

Regardless of the reasons for the hunger for vitamin D, I, like many of you, am happier when the sun comes out.

As a child I was the dark one. I was the kid who was scrubbed to raw flesh each night as my Mom assumed I was dirty. The tan started the first burst of spring and deepened with every day that followed until the dark veil of November dropped. There was no such thing as sunscreen; hats were for nerds or grandmothers; and sunglasses were for celebrities, or those who thought they were. And we were way too busy to ever stop long enough to lounge, bask or worship the sun. We just took it granted as our companion while we played.

By my teen years that all changed. Suddenly a tan represented a lifestyle. It meant you enjoyed the *good life* of fun, activity, beauty and prosperity ... or at least that's what the Bain de Soleil ads led us to believe. And so we baked our skin at any opportunity, any time of day, day of the week or month of the year. We craved the sun on our bodies, mostly because of the effect it had on it. Our badge of distinction was the achievement of the Coppertone tan.

Picture this typical scenario from my youth: sitting in Latin class, mid-February with the first hint of sunshine bursting through the cold barrier. From the back of the room I'd vacillate from looking up towards the nun to staring out at the sun. From the nun to the sun and back again, I sat tormented by my inner desire to flee. With a burst of courage and a bit of dramatics I'd work my way to the front of the room.

"Excuse me Sister, but I'm not feeling very well. May I please be excused?"

"Oh dear. Are you alright? Will you be OK tomorrow for the quiz?"

"Sister I'll not only feel better but I'm gonna look better too."

"Well then yes you are excused. Please take yourself right down to the nurses' office and get some rest."

"Thank you Sister. I will."

As the classroom door hit my backside, I leapt across the hall to the English class. Peering through the small window I would beckon for someone to bring me the baby oil. With coveted oil in hand, I'd run down to the cafeteria to beg for a sheet of aluminum foil. I'd line my Latin book with the aluminum foil, hike up my skirt, lower my socks and lather myself with Johnson's 'best'.

Next stop was out into the winter freshness and over to the sheltered alcove. And there I'd plop myself down protected from the air, but prime target for the sunshine as I subjected myself to the not yet harmful effects of the rays. With foil lined book in hand I remained aptly positioned for maximum reflection·of the sun on my face.

At this point in reading, if you're under 40 perhaps you scream, "BUT WHY? Did you not ever think of the risks you took and the damage you did?"

Well, that answer is simple. "No. Because I must admit, in ignorance, that our passion for the sun stems from the ardent belief that tanned fat just looks way better than white fat."

And if you feel the need to challenge that theory consider this fictional yet oh-so-close-to-real scenario:

It's early March. Vacation is coming and I'm going to an all inclusive. It's time to pack. I rummage through my last season's wardrobe cursing, "How is it my clothes seem to shrink in my closet? I wore these capris just four months ago and now I can't even do them up?"

Disappointed that last minute shopping would be mandatory I realize I better try on the bathing suit. As I reach for it and yank it from the lower drawer I bow my head in gratitude for the discovery of the all stretch, all forgiving fabric of Lycra.

I step into the suit and pull it over roll number one, number two, number three and four. As I pick, pull and poke it into position I catch sights of myself from various angles in the mirror and outwardly express my horror ... that three way mirror will have to go. I have been duped. Just last summer I paid big bucks for the miracle suit tagged with Tummy Minimizer. I realize now it's a fraud and discover the truth ... when it boasts Tummy Minimizer, it merely means it's a Butt Enhancer. The fat has got to go somewhere. Likewise if it brags Breast Minimizer, you will look like a bodybuilder as your breasts get mushed and pushed under your armpits.

Staring with sadness at the sight, I yell for Joe to solicit his honest opinion (a no-win predicament for any male). As Joe enters the room and catches sight of me his body does a 'Kramer' jerking with alarm at what he sees.

I whine, "Joooooooooe. How do I look?"

With a wince he hesitantly responds, "You look fine. You won't know anyone there."

Joe learned that diplomacy from my dad, who when asked "How do I look?" His typical response was, "You look fine. It'll be dark there."

Travel day approaches and the destination is an all-inclusive week-long vacation to Punta Cana. I pack layers of clothing for maximum protection fearful someone might actually take the time to look at me and my body (even though I try to believe that others are really too concerned about their own looks to be concerned about mine). I secretly hit the beach at five a.m. for early sun, away from the crowds. With each day I expose a little bit more skin slowly glowing a deeper shade of 'tan'.

Sitting upright from under the shade of the palm trees I watch the steady stream of bodies stroll the beach ... women sporting beaded braids in their sunburned parted hair, some flaunting their young bods in short shorts sitting above the butt line embroidered with Punta Cana, and older women defying gravity as they parade topless with their breasts so high they appear to be walking their owners. I sit in awe and wonder if I too might ever have the courage.

By Wednesday my exposure to the sun has lengthened. And when not lounging, I hit every a buffet and willingly accept every free drink extended in my direction. I'm grateful I packed the super-size Slurpee bottle,

By Thursday, my courage increases as my tan deepens.

By Friday, I unwrap the layers and proudly prance through the lobby, making a brief stop in the gift shop. I purchase my own pair of those cute little shorts ... too bad mine read the wide version of Punta Cana, The Dominican Republic. Next I visit the 'beach bead babes' and ask for extensions and beads for my own short white hair. I'm growing stronger, bolder and feel a whole lot better about myself.

By Saturday, with tan firmly in place I now confidently sit on the beach with nothing on but my bathing suit. I look around knowing I look better than *that one* and than *the one over there* and for sure *this one walking towards us right now.*

And who cares if I've gained 12 pounds. I feel good. The tan has boosted my mood and my confidence ... and suddenly I too want to walk the beach topless. Fat? What fat? I can't see any. The cellulite has been perfectly masked by the added colour. I'm certain it has disappeared altogether.

But again you cry "BUT WHY? I don't get it."

"It's easy." I reply. "When the sun comes out we just feel better about everything."

So after a spring doused with regular rainfalls I yearn for the warm breath of sunshine on my skin. I will once again face it and embrace it. BUT for my health and safety sake, it won't be before I lather my skin with sunscreen #60, retrieve my oversized hat and reach for the sunglasses large enough to fill half my face ... all for maximum protection from its harmful effects.

If it ever does come out again, I'll be ready. And I hope you will be too.

P.S. My dad, who was called Snowball because of the darkness of his Italian skin, was diagnosed with skin cancer in his 70's. None of us are safe.

Told Ya

In the early years of our marriage, Joe and I were always up for a trip during March Break, no matter what form. With children nowhere on the radar screen, it was easy to be spontaneous with our plans. Just two days before the start of one such break, Joe came home with a great offer. Friends had invited us to join them at their parents' trailer in Florida. The plan would be to fly stand-by out of Buffalo, spend the week with them in a one-bedroom trailer and pick up a drive-away car to return home. It wasn't the Ritz but it sounded like fun.

After failing to get a seat on the first two flights and spending the night in the airport, I looked forward to a relaxing week. I thought of the time we would spend lounging and meeting new people, and was eager to experience once again the excitement that's always in the air in Florida during spring break.

When we finally arrived at the trailer park we had a good look around, and immediately began to wonder if we would meet anyone under sixty-five. It was called Winterhaven, because it was obviously a haven for anyone in the winter of their life. Average age was 75 with skin like alligators.

As for the accommodation, let's simply say that Joe owed me big time for enduring this one. We shared a cot in the closet sized living room. To use the washroom we had to sneak through the master bedroom, quietly passing our friends who were invariably joined together as one.

Outside the confines of the tiny trailer, we did manage to enjoy ourselves. But somehow it just wasn't enough to save the trip. By Friday we were all a little testy (okay the guys were testy and the girls were esty). I was particularly anxious for a good night's sleep, so we headed out earlier than planned to pick up our car. It wasn't until we got the keys that we learned about the restrictions. First, it was a two-door car (the four of us stood 5'11" to 6'1"). Secondly, we were not allowed to open the trunk, which meant that all of our belongings had to sit with us inside the car. How could this get worse?

We began the drive determined to beat all previous time heats of the usual twenty-four hour journey. We were trying to make *good time,* whatever that means. With all of us sharing the same miserable attitude, conversation was shamelessly loaded with whining, moaning and complaining.

Tension hung in every corner of our small vehicle. According to the guys, we made *pretty good time* traveling through Florida, which encouraged us all. As we approached the Georgia border, we made a pit stop for gas and a round of coffees. It was also time to change drivers. It was Joe's turn at the wheel.

Knowing about his tendency to have a lead foot, I issued a cautionary warning (with a wee hint of nagging) from the back seat. "Joe, remember that we're in the States. The speed limit's lower here. You can't afford to get stopped ... "

And just as he was about to inform me about how he felt about unsolicited comments from the back seat, we heard the insistent wail of a siren. A quick twist of our heads and we knew absolutely, no doubt, for sure, the state trooper wanted us! Anticipating my victorious reprimand (na, na, na, na na!), Joe stared at me through the rear view mirror and issued the wordless warning, "Don't you dare say anything!"

As the state trooper approached the car with rifle in hand, we knew it was serious. One night in jail or $75 cash were the only options out of this mess. Collectively, we scraped together $53. He took it and stashed it in his pocket.

We drove the next fourteen and a half hours, curled up amidst our bags and belongings in complete silence. Despite the memory of the train wreck of a vacation we had just endured, I was curiously comforted by the sweet refrain of 'told ya!' that skipped around silently inside my head, its existence undetectable to my fellow passengers and evidenced only by the slightest upturn at the corners of my considerably silent lips.

Cookie Jar Caper

I collect cookie jars. It started when my mother let me take the one from home, a wedding gift to her in 1946. It was of an oversized woman. Since then I have inherited some, bought some at garage sales and received many as gifts, both used and new. I even have a few that are just on loan. There are about twenty-two cookie jars in all and the various styles and characters lend a strong element of kitsch to our kitchen decor.

One day before Christmas many years ago, I was visiting my friend Dianne Brittain. As she served my coffee she brought a beautiful cookie jar to the table and uncapped it to reveal her homemade treats. As much as I was ready to munch, I found the jar even more appetizing.

It was a pig. I immediately started asking questions about it, but she seemed to downplay its value and her attachment to it. Hmmm, the evil wheels in my head started to turn.

As I was headed towards the door I decided the pig deserved a more cookie jar friendly home where it would be properly revered and surrounded by other ceramic friends. I did not consider my next move to be theft, more like a rescue. I tucked it under my coat and was out the door.

During our annual open house two weeks later, my friend Sue was intrigued with the array of characters atop my kitchen cupboards. She asked me about each one, where I got them, how old they were etc. I responded with pleasure about my adored collection (that I know my children will toss to the curb as soon as I'm gone). She pointed to the newly adopted pig and asked specifically about it. Laughing, I said, "Oh, that one belongs to Dianne. I got it last week when I was visiting her."

"She gave it to you?"

"Well not really. She doesn't know I have it."

"You mean you stole it?"

"NOOO, I rescued it from an unfriendly environment. It wasn't treasured over there like it is here."

She appeared unconvinced about my motives, but we were interrupted so the conversation ended there.

It was the next morning when I was cleaning up that I noticed the cookie jar was missing. I immediately followed up with Sue and also our friends the Bekkers but no one was prepared to come clean. They were all adamant that they had nothing to do with it going missing.

I started to get nervous. My original plan was to surprise Dianne in January after she had ample time to stew about its disappearance. Surely over the holidays she would have noticed it was gone. But before I could figure out what to do I started getting ransom notes. Each one was accompanied by a photo of the jar in captivity accompanied by instructions about where to go to retrieve yet another note.

I was really starting to feel guilty because I knew that I eventually had to admit my crime to Dianne. In February I finally approached her and said I had to tell her something. First, I had *taken* her cookie jar, and second, I no longer had it to give back. I explained my dilemma. Although only half amused, she told me to keep her informed about anything else that happened. I felt better that at least she was deriving some enjoyment from the frustration I was going through.

The notes went on for most of the year with not a hint as to who was in possession of the jar. All photos were perfectly set up so that no clues about the pig's whereabouts could be discerned. By the fall, things waned and I eventually forgot about it.

Then, on the day of my open house a year after the rescue, there was a knock at the door. When I answered it no one was there but a package was on the stoop.

I read the cryptic poem with interest. I remained mystified until the last couplet ... "I love you Carole, but I've really been smitten ... by my rightful owner ... Dianne Brittain.

The joke was on me, as she had reclaimed possession of the stolen pig a year ago and was the perpetrator behind the entire ransom campaign.

Justice had been served.

Too Friendly Fun Run

I claim to have organized one of the first ever Hospital Fun Runs, in 1977. Of course the term itself is an oxymoron today, but we did have fun back then. Due to the success of the first, many more followed with registrations growing in number each time.

Our largest was held in conjunction with our organization's 25th anniversary in 1983. Over 300 runners registered in all categories. We accounted for the speedsters, the joggers, the walkers, the wheelchairs and an open section for those using other means. It took a lot of organizing but it was worth it.

I knew that volunteers would be crucial to the success of the event. We met days before, reviewed the route, outlined the duties of each post and gave out souvenir t-shirts to everyone donating their time.

The start and finish line was setup on the roadway which ran alongside a section of the hospital and was right next to the entrance of the auditorium. Ordinarily this large room would be our meeting place post-run for breakfast and presentations, however it has already been booked that day by another group.

Once the race began, I rallied the finish line volunteers for some last minute instruction. I wanted them to know how important it was to recognize all participants rather than just the winners. It didn't matter how or in what state they finished, I wanted them cheering and encouraging every single person. We wanted to foster a positive, supportive and especially, a fun environment. They all nodded in agreement as they showed their excitement. They were ready and armed with their megaphones, clappers and whistles. We knew the magnitude of the outward recognition would spread as each participant came in.

I left the area to check on the breakfast preparation. In my mind I had estimated that the first and fastest runners should be due in at 10:20 a.m. at the earliest. I then headed back out towards the finish line in what should have been plenty of time to welcome the overall winner, as well as the first runners of each category to cross the finish line. But as I approached, I was surprised to hear my volunteers burst into a raucous display of hooting and hollering. I remember thinking it must be a practice round. Because, it would be impossible that anyone of any category could be finished, unless they took a wrong turn along the route. The shortest route was five miles. They must either be Olympic runners or, perhaps they cheated.

Just in case my own timing was off, I sprinted over to the finish line to be sure not to miss taking a picture of the winners. I looked for the runners. Interestingly, I couldn't see any. Yet, the cheering continued.

It didn't take long to determine where it was directed. Over on the sidewalk along side of the building, I saw the three groups of walkers. Each one seemed to be cowering in embarrassment from all of the unwarranted attention. They huddled behind each other and as the hoopla increased they walked closer and closer to the wall of the auditorium. I was curious of their shyness. They were clearly uncomfortable with the attention. I stood back for a different look at the scene. I just couldn't figure it out. Ten very long seconds elapsed and I continued to follow their every step towards the line. Six feet before the finish, they made a hasty left hand turn and dashed through the open doors to the auditorium.

I yelled after them, "But wait. Come back. You have to get your pictures taken." They ignored my pleas and *en masse*, disappeared into the building.

In all the frenzy around the planning of this special event, I had failed to investigate which group had scheduled their meeting that morning in the hospital auditorium. The *Anonymous Self Help Group* met every Sunday at 10:30 a.m. I'm certain they did not appreciate our over enthusiastic hospitality.

A Tad Too Sensitive

*Y*ears ago, my sister and I vacationed with our mom in New York City. We stayed in a quaint, three-level hotel. Our room was on the main level and to have breakfast, it meant taking the elevator just one floor up.

As the doors opened for us to enter, there stood a *little person*. Ordinarily, this would be uneventful as we are mature enough to accept the differences. But there was one problem. At times our mom can innocently make comments, that although never meant to be hurtful, can be easily misinterpreted. The situation had all the signs of possible trouble. (In defense of our mother who has always warned, "Go ahead and make fun of me, your day will come." Sadly our *days* have already arrived.)

From the moment the doors opened, my sister and I shared a worried glance. As our mother chatted away, we held our breath, praying that nothing inappropriate would emerge from her mouth. Oblivious to our concerns, she cheerfully gave voice to every thought in her head, without pausing to edit.

It started ... "Well I don't know why we're taking the elevator for such a *short* ride.

And I hope it's *not a big* breakfast. I just feel like having something *small*.

Maybe a *bit* of fruit and a *little* yogurt."

Thankfully, it was only a one-floor ride and the doors opened before more damage could be done. We exited as quickly as possible, wondering what expression might be focussed on our backs.

Hopefully, like our mother, the young woman hadn't noticed. Perhaps we shouldn't have either.

Sound Check

*F*or many years Lori, Cathy and I hosted a fundraiser for women called *Beat the Blahs*. It was always a quick sell, mostly because it offered a fun way to help survive the winter months. Listening to me speak was definitely the secondary draw.

But I took the responsibility seriously. I was determined to give the audience their money's worth each year. Because we mostly drew the same people I had the challenge of coming up with new material for each event. And I did it with pleasure. It was an opportunity for me to be creative and to remain fresh. However, I rarely used the material again, due to the fact that I often stepped over the line when it came to censorship.

In 2007 I decided my theme would be *Top Ten Tips for Beautiful Aging*.

In Part One, I had fun with nine of those steps and Part Two was all about Step Ten: The Importance of Fitness. In this segment I decided to trace the evolution of fitness from the 1950's to modern day. At that point in the presentation the women were having a blast. They really seemed to enjoy my antics, one-liners and props. In particular they laughed hysterically at the costume changes that accompanied my intro to each decade. I would retreat behind the curtain where Sue acted as my dresser. We had all the props and pieces laid out for each sequence with our goal being to do it as quickly as possible to avoid any lulls in the proceedings.

The first change involved squeezing into a corset from the 1950's. When I tried it on earlier for Joe, he raised his brow as far as it could go in approval. It fit me perfectly, as long as I avoided breathing, excitable movements and laughing. Behind the curtain we laughed until we choked. We just couldn't manage to squeeze my tits into that corset and the front zipper refused to go over my ribs. Surely I hadn't gained weight since the day before? After each round of changes we laughed harder and pretty much every one of my body parts came under verbal fire. Sue is funny enough to have her own show so you know we were enjoying ourselves mightily.

The show ended with a standing ovation and when I introduced Sue the applause escalated. The evening was a huge success and we were gratified knowing the women were going home happy. They loved their goody bags, had been thoroughly entertained and we made a lot of money for Wellspring.

It wasn't until we had the *postmortem* at the pub that we discovered the real highlight of the evening. Sure, they loved the sequence of the show, the variety of the material and the guts I showed in pulling it off. But the absolute best part of the evening had less to do with my onstage performance than with what was going on behind the curtain between costume changes. Apparently despite all our backstage organization and attention to detail we had forgotten to turn off my mic every time I left the stage.

My friends proceeded to recite snippets of the backstage dialogue between Sue and me. We high-fived each other as we laughed hysterically, recalling each of the behind-the-curtain segments.

I shook my head when I thought about all the hours that had gone into preparing the material only to provide the best entertainment when we weren't even paying attention.

The Helium High

$\mathcal{I}$ have always believed a job should be fun. If I can't enjoy my work, I find no reason to continue doing it. Sorry, but that's the way I see it.

Consequently, in any job I have ever had, I did my best to search for the pleasure. If I couldn't find it I'd create it. As Director of Public Relations at The Mississauga Hospital in the days of healthy budgets and happy staff, I found many opportunities to spread the fun around. My office was on the edge of the hub of the administrative staff. Their offices were stark, décor subdued and mood generally serene.

My office was none of that. On any day they could take a break in the middle of the serious and pressing matters before them and poke their head into my office. Regularly, visitors to the area would drop by just to see what interesting collection I was storing in any of the corners. That was where I kept such assorted things as pink flamingoes, banners, T-shirts and various boxes of promotional goodies. If ever an obscure item was needed my office was the first stop on the search. Just the way I liked it.

In deference to my neighbours I tried to keep the noise and laughter under control, not only to avoid disturbing those around me but also to dodge accusations like: "Nobody who's having that much fun can possibly be working!'

One of my responsibilities was to chair the annual United Way campaign. To do this took time, creativity and resourcefulness. This one particular year we planned an exceptional campaign that required us to have one hundred helium balloons for the kick-off. I asked my friend Lorraine to help and together we decided to do the job in my office since the helium tank was already there. So we did.

Quickly we developed a system for inflating them. I worked the balloon onto the nozzle, pumped it up then knotted it while Lorraine cut the strings and stood waiting to tie one to each balloon. Upon completion, up to the ceiling it would fly and join the others as they awaited their final destination of the celebration.

The more balloons we inflated the more space they took up in the office. We giggled with delight as we became more and more engulfed in the colourful display. At the same time we were very conscious about not creating too much of that disturbance I mentioned earlier. We tried our best to keep the noise down as the balloons went up, especially because there was a special meeting in the president's office. I didn't want to bother them nor make them envious of the fun they were missing.

Well, our task was near completion and the more we pressed that helium nozzle the more giddy we became. We finally finished and successfully managed to suppress the laughter somewhere within our pantyhose. (Perhaps we had inhaled too much helium.) Just the sight of 100 colourful balloons lining the entire ceiling of my office made us hysterical. The multitude of curled strings fell like a steady downpour into the room providing that festive touch.

Our next challenge was to determine what to do with them. Should we move them somewhere else? Should we just leave them in my office until they were needed? Should we call patient transportation for volunteers to help us relocate them? Still laughing we considered the various plans and decided it might be best to just go for coffee.

As we made our may down the hall we heard a pop. One of the balloons had expired. Oh well. We continued on our way. Then, another popped. We cringed behind our hand-covered mouths at the sound and knew we were then down to ninety-eight. Together we hoped the *suits* hadn't heard anything but just when we figured it was safe to continue there a string of one pop after another followed by another and another.

Knowing we were now in a crisis situation made us laugh even louder and before we knew it, the massive collection of balloons exploded around us like five-cent firecrackers.

By this time we were holding our breath between screams. When the administrative assistant finally opened the door to find out what was going on we could clearly see the row of suited administrators gazing down their noses in our direction. This only made us laugh so hard we started jostling each other. It took just a few seconds for the wave of helium to be inhaled by the others and soon the rest of them joined in on the fun.

We quickly realized that the mere contact of latex to the ceiling tiles created enough friction to pop each balloon. Within minutes all that lay before us was a mass of curled string gripping the belly button of each balloon as the rest of their limp bodies covered the floor. It was a sad sight.

We never did get to use the balloons for the kick-off, but that day we all benefitted: the president's meeting adjourned with success, the rest of us approached our tasks, and the remainder of the day with a smile; and here we are still chuckling about it.

Honoured Plaque

*J*oe's family and my mother's family come from a small town in Italy called Porto St. Giorgio. Therefore, their adopted hero is St. George. He's the one who rode the horse and carried the large spear. Many people from this seaport immigrated to Canada and settled in Southern Ontario.

Each spring a small committee of men organize a large Seafood Festival in honour of their hometown namesake. Its splendor matches that of an elaborate Italian wedding. It starts with a mid-afternoon mass followed by a reception, seven-course meal with wine at every table and liqueurs to help it all settle. Speeches are given in Italian. Weeping men recount memories of their past. Distinguished town folk are remembered and typically the organizer holds the mic ten minutes too long. The attentiveness of the guests usually dwindles as he wraps up his annual speech. Everyone is anxious to play Tombola (Italian Bingo) and waits with great anticipation for the door prizes to be awarded.

There is always a disc jockey who can be counted on to play both *The Tarantala* and *Jeremiah Was A Bullfrog* in the same set. The evening ends with a roasted pig on a spit, assorted salad, crusty buns and a dessert selection to make the weight watchers salivate.

This event has always been very important to Joe. He has not missed a year since the first event was held in 1976. His dad used to be on The Committee and since his death, Joe has replaced him in this honoured role.

At the 1982 Festiva, we sat at a table with Joe's dad, my parents and another couple. Conversation got around to the elaborate display of door prizes. There were small appliances, fabric, chairs and an assortment of gift certificates. The grand prize was a trip to Italy. Leaning prominently against the head table was the prize that caught my eye. It was a very large plastered plaque of St. George wildly riding his horse as he spears the guts out of a dragon beneath him. It measured 45" by 24". The colour was horrifically vivid. The tones were golden with orange and red hues for accent. It had a glazed finish ... as if it needed more attention.

I jabbed Joe in the side and snickered, "Wouldn't that look good over our fireplace?"

We devoured the meal and sat patiently for the formal proceedings to end.

It was time for the draw and I sat clutching my ticket because I almost always win something. The first few numbers were called but mine wasn't among them. However when my father-in-law Giorgio shouted out, "Oh boy! Thatsa me!" I knew our table had a winner.

We waited with interest to see what Giorgio had won. Having just bought a house Joe and I sure could've used one of those portable vacuums so we secretly hoped he would share his winnings with us.

As he approached the stage I saw two committee members hoist up the plaque and present it to Giorgio, now brimming with pride. How appropriate, his namesake. Where on earth would he put it? It took two men to carry the blessed thing.

Joe and I grinned widely as we cheered Giorgio's good fortune. I leaned over to Joe and whispered, "Thank goodness it wasn't our ticket!" No sooner had the words left my mouth when I felt a tap on my shoulder. It was Giorgio. Now having the attention of the entire room he proudly announced that he wanted us to have it for our new home. Joe squeezed his eyes shut. (This is always a signal that he is either going to cry or laugh uncontrollably.) As I swallowed the lump of laughter in my own throat I managed a sheepish, "Thank you" to Giorgio.

It was obvious, this gesture made him feel really, really good.

As Joe and I nudged one another below the table we politely listened to the comments of the other guests:

"Oh my, it's beautiful."

"What a keepsake!"

"Such a special remembrance of our heritage."

"It will look lovely in your living room."

We nodded and had the good manners to keep quiet.

We laughed most of the way home. It took the two of us to lift it into the house. To hang it would have taken a suspension bridge.

Our furnishings have often been described as eclectic but despite our usual open mindedness we never did give it an honoured position in our home.

The most daylight it saw from inside its carton was during Giorgio's rare visits when we gamely leaned it against the fireplace. He beamed with pride at the sight of it.

After Giorgio's death we realized what a coveted treasure this plaque would be to others from their Italian hometown. Joe graciously offered it to a relative and I believe it now has a home where it is properly loved.

My Mom's Favourite Finger

"My Mom's got this finger ... it's just like yours and mine
But hers does so many things ... it's why I wrote this rhyme.

For sure, it is her favourite ... well, I kind of like mine too
Except my Mom uses hers ... way more often than I do.

I always know the mood she's in ... by looking at that finger
It tells me when to get away ... and when to stay and linger.

She uses it to make a point ... oh, I can handle that
It's when she aims it at my face ... it's like a baseball bat.

She uses it to bring me back ... by giving it a jiggle
When I do something wrong ... it really starts to wiggle.

She uses it to poke around ... my mouth and ears and nose
And needs it as she plays ... little piggies with my toes.

She uses it to scratch my itch ... it really does the trick
And when it's used to tickle me ... I laugh until I'm sick.

She uses it to whoop-di-doo ... 'round and 'round it goes
And it really comes in handy ... to wipe my runny nose.

She uses it to send me off ... so often to my room
When there is no comb around ... my hair, it tries to groom.

She uses it to flick away .... the bugs when it is hot
And at times it taps a tune .... to a beat that she has got.

She uses it to think a thought ... as she pokes above her eye
And on it's own, it says hello ... to any passerby.

She uses it to hold her nose .... when there is a stink
And when she types, it jabs at keys ... faster than you think.

She uses it as a grip ... I hold it when we walk
It's gently used to lift my chin ... when wanting me to talk.

She uses it to carry bags ... heavy ones at that
And when she puts it to her lips ... it's not the time to chat.

She uses it on the phone ... for fun and other duties
And to cast the magic spell ... to ward off all the cooties.

She uses it to check for dust ... on our tables and our chairs
And to turn each page ... as she reads *Three Little Bears.*

She uses it as a brush ... when we paint with fingers
And as a wand to music ... as she tries to make us singers.

She uses it to check the wind ... to see which way it's going
And rests it beside her face ... when something is annoying.

She uses it for counting ... it's always number one
I think that's why she loves it ... I think I'm almost done.

But I know a use my mom does not ... it really is so simple
Place it sideways 'tween your teeth ... wait to feel the dimple.

You'll find if you look into the mirror ... in just a little while
The frown that was on your face ... is now a great, big smile.

*Written for my kids 1992

About Carole

Carole plays a multitude of roles in her busy life, the most important ones being with family and friends. Her personal credo includes the hierarchy of Faith, Family, Friends and ultimately FUN and especially enjoys when they meet.

Beyond that Carole (CBL) is self-employed as a professional speaker with her company CBL Presentations Inc. Known as The Moodivator, Carole is a Canadian Best-Selling Author of two books, a prolific blogger, a-not-quite-yet YouTube sensation and an eager participant in coffee dates.

Always willing to share her insight and two cents worth, Carole readily and frequently doles out her creative thoughts with the intent to benefit others. One of her dream jobs would be to offer services as The Thinking Cap, giving other needy entrepreneurs an opportunity to pick her over-active brain for creative and workable ideas. Stay tuned.

Carole balances her 'heads up' work as a speaker, with her other work, which requires her 'head down and butt up in the air' as the owner-operator of a family gardening business called Yard Duty.

Carole successfully blends the demands of her work with the pleasure of her play and is proud to admit they often overlap.

If you would like to check her out beyond what you have already learned about her in this book, there are plenty of opportunities. She's everywhere ...

www.carolebertuzziluciani.com (personal)

www.moodivator.ca (CBL Presentations)

www.ihaveastoryforyou.com (books)

www.moodivator.ca/blog (blogs)

www.youtube.com/moodivator (videos)

... & if that's not enough, there's always Facebook, Twitter or the old fashioned face to face connection ~!!~

"Thanks for your interest and your time ...
I sure hope you enjoyed the read."